Family Frolics
Relief Society Renditions
and Sharing Time Skits

Edited by C. Michael Perry

AUTHORS:
*Charlee Cardon Wilson, Sam Christensen,
Sharon Elwell, & James G. Lambert*

A collection of 16 short plays and skits
that can be easily produced for:
Primary Sharing Time
Family Home Evening
Sunday School Lessons
Relief Society Gatherings
Firesides
Ward & Stake parties
and other occasions

This book is to be used as a resource manual only. Individual copies of each skit are available from the publisher at a very small price per copy, plus postage and handling. (See order forms in back) No royalties will be charged if the required number of copies is purchased. Some of the skits have original music and well-known songs to go with them. This music is <u>not</u> included in this manual, but <u>is</u> included in the purchase of each script.

Zion Theatricals
in association with
Zion BookWorks
Salt Lake City

© 1995 & 2014 by C. Michael Perry (as a collection)
ALL RIGHTS RESERVED
CAUTION: Professionals and amateurs are hereby warned that
Family Frolics, Relief Society Renditions and Sharing Time Skits

being fully protected under the copyright laws of the United States Of America, the British Empire, including the Dominion Of Canada, and the other countries of the Copyright Union, is subject to royalty. Anyone presenting the play without the express written permission of the Copyright owners and/or their authorized agent will be liable to the penalties provided by law.

A requisite number of script and music copies must be purchased from the Publisher and Royalty must be paid to the publisher for each and every performance before an audience whether or not admission is charged. A performance license must first be obtained from the publisher prior to any performance(s).

Federal Copyright Law -- 17 U.S.C. section 504 -- allows for a recovery of a minimum of $250 and a maximum of $50,000 for each infringement, plus attorney fees.

The professional and amateur rights to the performance of this play along with the lecturing, recitation, and public reading rights, are administered exclusively through ZION THEATRICALS without whose permission in writing no performance of it may be made. For all other rights inquiries may be made to the authors through ZION THEATRICALS Any adaptation or arrangement of this work without the author's written permission is an infringement of copyright. **Unauthorized duplication by any means is also an infringement.**

FOR PUBLIC PERFORMANCE RIGHTS YOU MUST APPLY TO THE PUBLISHER OR YOU ARE BREAKING THE LAW!

The possession of this SCRIPT whether bought or rented, does not constitute permission to perform the work herein contained, in public or in private, for gain or charity. Proper prior application must be made and license granted before a performance may be given. Copies of this SCRIPT and all other rehearsal materials may be bought and/or rented from:

ZION THEATRICALS
3877 W. Leicester Bay South Jordan, UT 84095
www.ziontheatricals.com
Printed in the United States Of America

Whenever this play is produced the following notice should appear in the program and on all advertisements under the producer's control: "Produced by special arrangement with Zion Theatricals, South Jordan UT" In all programs and posters and in all advertisements under the producers control, the author's name shall be prominently featured under the title.

NOTE: Your contract with Zion Theatricals limits you to making copies of this document for persons directly connected with your production. Do not distribute outside of your cast and crew. Following your performance run you must destroy all photocopies, preferably by shredding them. If we sent you the document in printed format, you must return that document to us. If we provided you with an electronic PDF file, simply trash that on your computer so that it cannot be recovered. The electronic document may only be on ONE computer -- it may NOT be duplicated. This is also a part of your contract with Zion Theatricals.

NOTE: Each play is also individually copyrighted by its author, as noted in each individual script.

FAMILY FROLICS, RELIEF SOCIETY RENDITIONS & SHARING TIME SKITS

This collection of 16 skits, sketches, playlets and monologues is specifically designed for use as inservice lessons, Primary Sharing Time, Family Home Evenings, Priesthood, Relief Society or Sunday School lessons, Firesides, Young Mens and Women's classes and meeting nights, and other Ward and Stake presentations. These short plays (not longer than 20 minutes) are designed primarily to teach, in an interesting way, a single or group of related Gospel principles. Drama makes all things easily understandable and able to be grasped by anyone who is learning. They are easy to produce and very affordable. They can all be easily produced with a minimum of props and costumes and no setting. Or you can be as elaborate as you want. All of these short plays are published in a Resource Manual that is available to Church libraries or individuals at a cost of $8.95. Nothing may be photocopied out of the Resource Manual. It is against the law!!! The price of the Resource Manual does NOT include any production rights! A Production Package for each skit may be purchased at the listed price (below). Each Production Package purchase permits you to print a certain number of copies from the PDF original that will be emailed to you. The authors represented are: *Charlee Cardon Wilson, Sam Christensen, Sharon Elwell, & James G. Lambert.*

RESOURCE MANUAL CONTAINING ALL 16 SCRIPTS: $8.95 (Order # 4000)

No portion of this book may be reproduced in any form
Without written permission from the author's representative.

ZionBookWorks
3877 Leicester Bay South Jordan UT 84095
www.zionbookworks.com

First Edition by Leicester Bay Books (CS): 2014 --
ISBN-13: 978-0615999142
ISBN-10: 061599914X
NOOK Edition: 2014

Table Of Contents

AND THAT'S THE WAY IT WAS --
    by Charlee Cardon Wilson   1
    2 adults 2 children. Chairs only.

Uses well known Church folk tunes and the Walter Cronkite news format to explain about the pioneers to young audiences. About 15 mins. **Order # 4001. $7.50** for a Production Package that includes rights to duplicate 3 copies.

THE EXAMPLE --
    by Charlee Cardon Wilson   4
    4 women.

A short skit testifying that it's really not so hard to do a little missionary work. About 10 mins. **Order # 4002. $5.00** for a Production Package that includes rights to duplicate 4 copies.

FUNSMOKE --
    by Sam Christiansen   8
    7M 2W. 1 simple set.

A spoof of "Gunsmoke". The narrator is the only one prepared in advance. The costumes are brought, the cast is selected from the audience, costumed and handed scripts. They may be coached if desired. A great ice-breaker for Ward and Stake functions. A lot of silly fun. The whole process takes about 15 mins. **Order # 4003. $7.50** for a Production Package that includes rights to duplicate 9 copies.

THE IGI CAPER --
    by Charlee Cardon Wilson   13
    2M 1W 1B + group of 6 readers.

A readers theatre piece using the "Dragnet" TV format to uncover clues as to how to pursue one's genealogy. About 15 mins. **Order # 4004. $7.50** for a Production Package that includes rights to duplicate 10 copies.

JONAH AND THE BIG FISH --
    by Sharon Elwell   19
    4M + extras.

The Bible story retold for Primary. It can use children or adults to tell the story. The props and the costumes are the important things to prepare in advance. Action can be improvised. About 10 mins. **Order # 4005. $5.00** for a Production Package that includes rights to duplicate 5 copies.

LET FREEDOM RING --
a skit with original music by Charlee Cardon Wilson   22
1 female adult, 5 mixed youth.

A testimony builder about the freedom we all need in our spiritual as well as our temporal lives. About 20 mins. **Order # 4006. $10.00** for a Production Package (with music) that includes rights to duplicate 6 copies.

MALADIES PECULIAR TO THE MORMON FAITH --
by Charlee Cardon Wilson   31
5 non-speaking female roles, 3 or 4 mixed speaking roles.

Just some of the "illnesses" we "Saints" fall prey to. Very funny and easy to do. About 10 mins. **Order # 4007. $5.00** for a Production Package that includes rights to duplicate 3 copies.

NEPHI AND LABAN --
by Sharon Elwell   36
8 speaking roles, several non-speaking roles.

Another skit for young people telling how Nephi obtained the brass plates. Can be done impromptu with only props and costumes prepared ahead of time. **Order # 4008. $7.50** for a Production Package that includes rights to duplicate 8 copies.

THE NO TALENT --
by Charlee Cardon Wilson   40
1 female.

A monologue designed to enable people to think about their own self-worth. About 10 mins. **Order # 4009. $5.00** for a Production Package that includes rights to duplicate 2 copies.

PIONEER CHILDREN --
by Charlee Cardon Wilson   44
2 male youth, 2 female youth, 1 boy, 1 girl.

Using the youth we and they learn a little bit about what the pioneer youth had to endure. About 20 mins. **Order # 4010. $10.00** for a Production Package that includes rights to duplicate 7 copies.

THE RELUCTANT SHEPHERD --
by James G. Lambert.   54
2 men, 2 women, 2 boys, 2 girls + angels and other shepherds.

A story behind the "no room at the inn" story. A young shepherd boy gives Mary and Joseph the use of his family's stable and manger without payment. He also furnishes them with the food that was to have been his family's first meal in several days. His family is furious with him until they see who the strangers in their stable are. About 20 mins. **Order # 4011. $10.00** for a Production Package that includes rights to duplicate 8 copies.

VISITING TEACHING LEADER --

by Charlee Cardon Wilson   **59**

1 female narrator, 4 non-speaking females.

Describes in delightful detail some of the different types of Visiting Teachers. About 10 mins. **Order # 4012. $5.00** for a Production Package that includes rights to duplicate 2 copies.

A VOICE FROM THE DUST --

A skit with original music by Charlee Cardon Wilson   **65**

2M 1narrator, optional chorus.

The use of slides, drama and song to tell of the downfall of the Nephites under Moroni, his vision to Joseph Smith and the founding of the Church in the Latter-day. About 20 mins. **Order # 4013. $10.00** for a Production Package that includes rights to duplicate 3 copies. (Slides come from building libraries)

THE PUMPKIN CHILD --

A puppet or live action skit with original music   **70**

1 M 6F 1 either

This little musical sketch is about loving and respecting others. About 15 minutes. With original songs. **Order #4014. $10.00** for a Production Package that includes rights to duplicate 11 copies.

SOCKY AT THE DENTIST --

A very short skit   **74**

2 puppets

A little bit of silly fun with maybe a moral? About 2 minutes. **Order #4015. $3.00** for a Production Package that includes rights to duplicate 2 copies.

FAMILY COUNCIL IN HEAVEN --

A skit for puppets or people   **75**

3M 1W 5 either

What happened in that Council and how it affected all of us. About 6-7 minutes. Order #4016. $7.50 for a Production Package that includes rights to duplicate 10 copies.

Individual copies of each script are printed in 8 1/2 x 11 inch, PDF format. If original music is available it is included with each script.

HOW TO ORDER

1. Telephone orders may be placed by calling 801-550-7741. OR you can e-mail "cmichaelperry53@gmail.com". Payment can be by check or through PayPal. We will send the material to you through your e-mail.
2. An order form is provided at the back of this resource manual, if you need it. All orders must be paid for prior to delivering the material to you through your email address.

REMEMBER: you may <u>not</u>, in any way, copy or reproduce the play/skits in this manual. <u>Nor</u> may you copy or reproduce any of the material you order from this manual, without paying the nominal fees. If you do so you will be breaking the law and are subject to fines and fees! If you happen to lose your PDF file, we will gladly replace it, once it has been paid for. Please contact us to obtain the copy needed. Be safe! Don't break the law! Copying books in whole or in part <u>robs</u> the author of his livelihood and is illegal and immoral.

Index to the skits by Topic
(M) = has songs, (w/S) uses slides(or other video/projections)

Bible
Jonah & The Big Fish

Book of Mormon
Nephi & Laban
Voice From The Dust, A (M)

Christmas
Reluctant Shepherd, The (w/S)

Church History
And That's The Way It Was
Pioneer Children (w/S)
Voice From The Dust, A (M)

Dinners & Socials
Funsmoke
Reluctant Shepherd, The (w/S)
Voice From The Dust, A (M)
The Pumpkin Child (M)

Family Home Evening
And That's The Way It Was
Family Council In Heaven
Jonah & The Big Fish
Maladies Peculiar To The Mormon Faith
Nephi & Laban
The Pumpkin Child (M)
Socky At The Dentist

Firesides
Example, The
IGI Caper, The
Maladies Peculiar to the Mormon Faith
No-Talent, The
The Pumpkin Child (M)
Reluctant Shepherd, The
Voice From The Dust, A (M)

Genealogy
IGI Caper, The

Missionary
Example, The
Voice From The Dust, A (M)

Patriotic (24th July Also)
And That's The Way It Was
Let Freedom Ring (M)
Pioneer Children (w/S)

Primary
And That's The Way It Was (w/S)
Family Council In Heaven
Jonah & The Big Fish
Nephi & Laban
Pioneer Children
The Pumpkin Child (M)
Reluctant Shepherd, The
Socky At The Dentist

Relief Society
And That's The Way It Was (w/S)
Example, The
Maladies Peculiar To The Mormon Faith
No-Talent, The
Visiting Teaching Leader

Self-Worth
No-Talent, The
The Pumpkin Child (M)

Sunday School
And That's The Way It Was (w/S)
IGI Caper, The
Pioneer Children
Voice From The Dust, A (M)

Visiting Teaching
Visiting Teaching Leader, The

Young Men/Young Women
Funsmoke
IGI Caper, The
Let Freedom Ring (M)
Pioneer Children
Voice From The Dust, A (M)

Family Frolics, Relief Society Renditions and Sharing Time Skits -- Resource Manual

AND THAT'S THE WAY IT WAS!
by Charlee Cardon Wilson

CHARACTERS
--SEVERAL CHILDREN (Non speaking -- if desired)
--TEACHER
--PIONEER MOTHER
NOTE:
The songs used in this skit are taken from the seminary book of LDS folk songs. Check your ward library for copies of the songs.

Teacher is seated stage left. Children may be seated in chairs on either side of her, or she may treat the audience as her "children". Other stage setting should reflect a Primary class atmosphere. Use a table and easel if desired. Leave room stage right for pioneer woman (Mother) to enter Use a spotlight to follow speakers if one is available. Teacher is too sweet, a caricature.

TEACHER: Now boys and girls, today our lesson is about the pioneers. How many of you had pioneer ancestors? Oh my, I can see you probably know a lot about pioneers already. Now let's just pretend a moment that we lived back in those exciting times. Can you think how marvelous it must have been to see the beautiful Salt Lake Valley for the first time. The pioneers were so happy to finally reach their destination. They could hardly wait to build their houses and plant their gardens. Let's imagine we're pioneers with our hand cart, pushing and pulling our way to the top of the hill where we can see our new home.
    (She gets into the spirit, pantomiming pushing.)
I'm so happy. Let's sing a song as we push, all right?
    (Audience joins in singing from printed song sheets.)

SOME MUST PUSH AND SOME MUST PULL

    (Enter pioneer mother, hot and tired, babe in arms, one toddler at her skirts and one obviously on the way.)
MOTHER: This is the place? Are you sure?.....Gee, I don't doubt that we can make this desert bloom, it's just....well... I guess I didn't expect to start from scratch is all... And Hyrum, dear Hyrum...where are you when I need you? You're off spreading the gospel to those folks back home...trying to bring them out of darkness into the light. Trying to point the way to Zion....And this is Zion? Oh Hyrum, my mother tried to warn me.
    (She sings. She may be joined by other pioneer mothers if desired. If so, they

all enter with her and stay in the background until song begins. Seat some and have some stand as she speaks. They exit with her.)

THE MORMON BOYS

MOTHER: Well, come on, Hannah.
(Takes toddler's hand)
Papa's toiling in the Lord's vineyard. He'll be sending folks to join us in this new land of milk and honey. There's work to be done before they arrive.
(Exit.)

TEACHER: Boys and girls, did you know that not all the pioneers stayed in Salt Lake City. Not long after they came to the Salt Lake Valley, President Brigham Young called some of them to continue on to other places to settle. So some of the pioneers got to go on another exciting journey. Let's pack up our handcarts and pretend we're going along with them. I'm so excited to be traveling again, I feel like singing. Let's sing like the pioneers did.
(Audience sings second verse with teacher.)

SOME MUST PUSH AND SOME MUST PULL

MOTHER: *(Enters with a bucket that she's putting buffalo chips in. She bends, picks one up and puts it in bucket. She wipes her hands on her apron and looks around. If desired, other women can also be gathering chips and join her in the song.)* If anybody ever told me that I'd be excited about an abundance of buffalo chips I'd have.....oh well...I wonder if the radishes I planted before we left are ready yet. I hope Sister Sorenson appreciates that little garden patch I left behind. When that little twig of an apple tree shot out those four leaves, I almost cried with joy. Now, here I am again....Dixie. I wish I had Brother Brigham's faith. 'Pears to me this place must have been over-looked during the Creation. It just doesn't look....finished. And Hyrum, there you go again. Off without purse or scrip and leaving me the same. Ah well, we do have some good times...like last night's social. Brother Smith is such a wit! How did his song go?...
(She sings, joined by others if desired.)

COTTONWOOD

(Mother and others exit as spotlight comes up on Teacher.)

TEACH: You know, many of the pioneers spent their lives settling first one place and then another. They'd no sooner build a house and plant a garden, then it would be time to move on to a new location. It was a happy, busy time. They sang as they traveled along. At night, they gathered around the campfire and sang and danced and told stories. Let's pretend we're singing around the campfire.

(Audience joins Teacher and sings third verse of song.)

SOME MUST PUSH AND SOME MUST PULL

MOTHER: (Enters and appears older. Do this with a quick touch of white in the hair, a few lines on her face and a slightly stooped posture. A cane is a nice addition. If others are used, pose them as in a street scene.) Well, well, will you look at that...I do believe old St. George is finally beginning to look like more than just a collection of shacks. We've managed to raise some cotton and some fruit. My garden has been so good these last years. Even Hyrum got in on this last move. I hope I'm not tempting fate when I say "last move". I'm ready to settle down and stay put...even in St. George. Oh, it isn't so bad now, but oh do I remember those first years....
    (Sings)

ST. GEORGE AND THE DRAG-ON

TEACHER: *(Mother freezes)* And that, boys and girls, is the way it was in the happy, exciting times of our pioneer ancestors!
    (Audience sings final chorus joined by pioneer Mother and any others used. Or, if desired, close curtain after teacher's final speech.)

(THE END)

THE EXAMPLE
by
Charlee Cardon Wilson

CHARACTERS
    Bright Light
    Dim Bulb
    Mary Jane
    Anna Jack

May be set in chapel using chairs on the stand, or on stage with simple props to look like a waiting room. Avoid the Doctor's office look. Use the Stake President's office as a model. As the scene begins, Dim Bulb is seated in waiting room. You may wish to dress all characters in white, but Sunday clothes would also be appropriate. Light colors work better than dark, however.

    BRIGHT LIGHT: *(Enters cheerfully)* Hi, am I in the right place? I'm supposed to have an interview with St. Peter.

DIM BULB: For your Celestial Recommend'?
    (BRIGHT LIGHT nods)
Yes, well, this is the place, as they say. I'm waiting for mine too.

BRIGHT LIGHT: *(Sits down)* Enjoy, am I nervous! This is my first interview for a Celestial Recommend. Is it very difficult

DIM BULB: Actually, it's my first time too.
    (Enter Mary Jane)

MARY JANE: Well, well, look who's here
    (Goes to BRIGHT LIGHT and shakes her hand)
Betcha don't remember me.

BRIGHT LIGHT: Well.u..I....uh...

MARY JANE: Mary Jane Campbell, remember....third grade. You used to take me to Primary with you.

BRIGHT LIGHT: Oh, for heaven's sake! Yes! I do remember How are you

MARY JANE: Oh, I'm just fine. Just got back from a mission to the Spirit Prison. You know, it's so much harder for our investigators here than it is on the other side I'm sure glad I got my work done before I came....Oh, you didn't know, did you I joined the Church So did my husband

BRIGHT LIGHT: Terrific! I'll bet the missionaries were delighted to find you.

MARY JANE: Oh, the missionaries didn't find us. I found them. See, when my kids were young, they started asking questions about Jesus. I couldn't answer most of them. In fact, the answers I did have were all from Primary, So, I figured I'd let Primary give my little ones the answers too. When I saw what a change it made for the kids, I decided to see if the adult programs were as good....just for the social side, of course. Funny, I got that same sort of peaceful glow inside that I used to get when you took me to Church. It was like coming home again. Well, you know....

BRIGHT LIGHT: Yes I do know. I just never can express it very well.

MARY JANE: Are you here for your interview?

BRIGHT LIGHT: Yes, and am I nervous! Neither one of us has ever had one before.

DIM BULB: I've heard he's pretty tough.

MARY JANE: Well, I guess so. But he's fair, and as long as you've been making the effort...you know, tithing, loving your neighbor, missionary work, etc., you'll do okay...I'd better dash. I have to go report. Good seeing you.

BRIGHT LIGHT: Bye.....

(Mary Jane exits)...

Oh dear, I wonder how strict the rules are on missionary work.

DIM BULB: Just a trace of self-righteousness Actually, I never found missionary work difficult.

BRIGHT LIGHT: Oh? Did you ever bring anyone into the Church? I under stand that's the greatest feeling in the world!

DIM BULB: Well, I can't say that I actually ever converted anyone, but I certainly did my best to set a good example for my non-member friends. You now, to show them how full the gospel plan makes your life. I used to tell my neighbor that she wouldn't need PTA, Brownies, Symphony Guild, o any of the dozens of community organizations she belonged to if she was a member of my church. She said she couldn't afford the time to be a Mormon if it meant being as busy as I was..I was always going out the door to one meeting or another...You know, it's sad, but some people are just too tied up in busy work to consider their own salvation.

(Enter Anna Jack.)

ANNA JACK: Why, look who's here! How are you dear?

(Goes to BRIGHT LIGHT and gives her a hug.)

BRIGHT LIGHT: Well, hello, Sister Jack! How are you?

ANNA JACK: Busy, as usual. Remember Eloise?

(BRIGHT LIGHT nods)

I'm on my way over to see her Her temple work is being done today. She's been waiting so long.

BRIGHT LIGHT: But, I thought she'd joined the church.

ANNA JACK: She did. She was called home before she got her endowments. There was no one in her family to get them done until recently

BRIGHT LIGHT: Oh, that's right! Well, who is having the work done now

ANNA JACK: Her daughter, Laura. Remember her?

BRIGHT LIGHT: Of course. We used to go the the genealogy library together. In fact, once she'd found out that our branch library was open to everyone, she used it more than any of the members did. She even used to come with me to Sunday School to attend the genealogical class. I'm ashamed to say that's as brave as I ever got. I never even asked her the golden questions.

ANNA JACK: Well, something made an impression She's teaching that genealogical class now and is in charge of expanding the branch library. She was baptized about a year ago. Of course, Eloise is delighted and so are a lot of other folks who've been waiting on someone to send in their records...I'd better run Can't wait to break the news.

BRIGHT LIGHT: Oh, be sure and say "hello" to Eloise for me
(Anna JACK waves and exits.)

DIM BULB: Who was that?

BRIGHT LIGHT: Oh, I'm sorry. I should have introduced you She used to be my neighbor. We shared a sort o garden plot between our two houses. Her husband wasn't a member, and she wasn't active. Relief Society changed that. We'd had a bumper crop of zucchinis and were frankly sick of it. Then, I found out that our Homemaking meeting was doing a tasting table on zucchini, so I asked her to come. Well, she wouldn't go, but I brought samples of everything home for her to taste. She was impressed. After that she said she'd like to go to some of the cooking classes sometime. I started giving her her our Relief Society newsletter that told all the up-coming classes She came to a couple o cooing classes, then she saw a mini-class on sewing coming Up and she came with me to that too. Pretty soon, she was attending all the homemaking meetings and even bringing some of her non-member friends with us. Eloise was one of them. She and another lady joined the church We moved shortly afterwards, but I heard that Sister Jack had been put in as Homemaking counselor and that her husband was taking the lessons.

DIM BULB: Did you ever ask m the golden questions when you lived so close?

BRIGHT LIGHT: Oh no. I was simply too chicken. I guess I was afraid of offending him

DIM BULB: Well, the way I always looked at it was, if the golden questions offended anyone, that was their problem. I'd done my part I wouldn't be held accountable.

BRIGHT LIGHT: I guess you were never afraid to ask the golden questions

DIM BULB: Heavens no!...I asked them many times. The trick is in the approach. For instance, my next door neighbor was a widow and a diabetic. One Christmas, I baked a pumpkin pie for her. I figured she couldn't very well bake one herself with her diabetes and all, and that she'd probably appreciate something on hand to give her holiday guests that drop in. When I delivered it I asked her the golden questions.

BRIGHT LIGHT: What did she say? Did she take the lessons?

DIM BULB: Oh, she said she wasn't interested, but sometimes you have to plant the seeds and give them time to sprout. I left her our meeting schedule and directions on how to find the building if she changed her mind.

BRIGHT LIGHT: And did she?

DIM BULB: No, there was a lot of snow that year, and she just hated driving in the snow.or at least that's what she said. some seeds just fall on infertile ground. You have to accept that sometimes. Of course, you don't always have to be so direct with people either. Sometimes it's better to be subtle..like, one Halloween, I gave all the trick or treaters little Article of Faith cards instead of candy. And, when my husband's secretary had her baby, I sent her a Book of Mormon with the baby's name printed on the cover...Strangest thing, I never received a thank you note for that....I also sent a Church News subscription to all my husband's best customers at Christmas time too.

BRIGHT LIGHT: *(Sighs enviously)* My, you have a lot of courage!

DIM BULB: No not really, it's easy when you know you're doing what you've been commanded to do. Missionary work is really a snap!

(Snaps fingers.)
BLACKOUT

(THE END)

Family Frolics, Relief Society Renditions and Sharing Time Skits -- Resource Manual

FUNSMOKE
by Sam Christensen

CAST
THE NARRATOR

PEOPLE CHOSEN ON THE SPOT
MATTHEW DILLY -- The Marshall
PESTUS HAYSTACK -- The Deputy
DOC -- The Town Doctor
MS. CAT -- Owner of the A & W Saloon
JACK S. BLACKHEART -- the bad guy
PEDRO -- Jack S.'s sidekick
PANCHO -- Pedro's sidekick

PRODUCTION NOTE: Before hand the director should gather costumes and props and have everything ready to give each character before the performance. The NARRATOR should be the only one that you "rehearse" with. He/she should be familiar with the action and flow of the story so that he/she can facilitate the performance. Once the actors are chosen out of the audience they can be coached and they might even have time to glance through the script and prepare their bits minutes before their performance. Most important -- HAVE FUN!!!

PROLOGUE
NARRATOR: A real life drama of what life was really like in the real live West when life was really tuff! Matthew Dilly -- big, tall, handsome, strong U.S. Marshall with white teeth, white hat and black, patent leather size 16 waffle stompers. He carries a .44 with a 24 inch barrel and voted Democrat in the last election. There is only one true love in his life -- himself!
   (ENTER MATTHEW)
Pestus Haystack -- dumb, ugly, stupid and voted Republican. He idolized Dilly (but so does everyone) . He has bad breath, food stamps, BO, whiskers, poor English and morning back ache from sleeping on a too soft mattress.
   (ENTER PESTUS)
Doc -- Town Doctor, a veter'narian, butcher, wallpaper hanger and sells A&W Root Beer part time. He has a wrinkled vest, dirty fingernails, a monthly Army retirement check and a golf handicap of 16.
   (ENTER DOC)
Ms. Cat -- The owner of the local A&W Saloon. She is petite for a 6'4" half-

back, dainty with size 14 Army boots and has a pleasant smile with three teeth missing. She is secretly in love with Dilly (but so is everyone else). She does part time go-go dancing for the (NAME SOME LOCAL THEATRE) theatre.
 (ENTER MS. CAT)
Jack S. Blackheart -- (commonly called "Ole Jack S.) Mean, bad, ugly, dirty, and generally unpleasant. He robs banks, shoots homesteaders, rustles cattle, steals horses, and works part time in a flower shop. His boots are too tight, his underwear makes him itch, his hat gives him a headache and his wife gives him a pain in the neck.
 (ENTER JACK S.)
Pedro -- Ole Jack S.'s sidekick. Short, stupid, ignorant, and has a degree in sociology from the (LOCAL UNIVERSITY) He speaks 13 languages, plays center for the Boston Celtics and runs a trading post at (LOCAL INDIAN RESERVATION OR NATIONAL PARK)
 (ENTER PEDRO)
Pancho -- Pedro's sidekick. Shorter, stupider and ignoranter than Pedro. He teaches Math, Home-Ec. and Ping-pong at the (LOCAL TRADE SCHOOL OR JR. COLLEGE)
 (ENTER PANCHO)
Miss Fifi -- Go-go dancer at Ms. Cat's A&W. She is small, pretty, cute, petite and speaks French with a Texas accent. She is Ole Jack S.'s girl and plays goalie for the Chicago Black Hawks.
 (ENTER MISS FIFI)

ACT ONE --

NARRATOR: The scene is the main cafeteria of Ms. Cat's A&W on the back street of Dog City in the Old West when these great Americans were pushing westward, exploring the vast frontier, conquering the unknown, suffering hardship, want and hunger, in constant fear of Indian attack, to make this the great country they want their children to grow up in, free from hardship, want, hunger and Indian attack.
 (DOC AND PESTUS ARE SITTING AT THE TABLE DRINKING A LARGE LIME FLAVORED CHERRY CHOCOLATE DR. PEPPER WITH ORANGE SHERBET AND A CHERRY AND ARGUING)
Doc says
DOC: Oh yeah.
NARRATOR: Pestus counters
PESTUS: Oh yeah.
NARRATOR: Doc says with authority
DOC: Oh yeah.
NARRATOR: Pestus says stupidly

PESTUS: Oh yeah.
NARRATOR: Doc says humbly
DOC: Oh yeah.
NARRATOR: Pestus smiles and says
PESTUS: Oh yeah.
NARRATOR: Ms. Cat enters with two new drinks.
MS. CAT: Oh yeah.
NARRATOR: Miss Fifi enters and sits on Pestus's lap.
MISS FIFI: *(WITH FRENCH ACCENT)* Oh yeah.
NARRATOR: Doc pouts
DOC: Oh yeah.
NARRATOR: Dilly enters in all his glory and announces
DILLY: Oh yeah.
> *(HE WALKS OVER AND PUSHES PESTUS OFF HIS CHAIR, SETS DOWN AND SETS FIFI ON HIS LAP)*

PESTUS: Thanks, I needed that.
> *(ENTER JACK S., PEDRO & PONCHO LOOKING MEAN, NASTY AND UNHAPPY)*

NARRATOR: Jack S. growls
JACK S: I'm going to rob the bank, shoot five homesteaders, steal four horses and track mud on your floor.
PEDRO: Hasta la vista.
PANCHO: Si.
NARRATOR: Jack S. proclaims
JACK S: I'm going to rustle some cattle, rob the stage and tip over the out house.
PEDRO: Manana.
PANCHO: Si.
NARRATOR: Jack S. threatens
JACK S: I'm going to burn the General Store, scalp the Devere Walker and drink all the A&W Root Beer.
PEDRO: Acapulco.
PONCHO: Si.
NARRATOR: Dilly stands up magnificently and says
DILLY: Oh yeah.
NARRATOR: Jack S. replies nastily
JACK S: Oh yeah.
PEDRO: Guadalajara.
PANCHO: Si.
> *(MISS FIFI SCREAMS AND RUNS OUT OF THE ROOM)*

NARRATOR: Enter Henry Kissinger and they all sit down and start discussing their differences calmly, Ms. Cat serves all Root Beer Floats. As the scene closes all are singing "Onward Christian Soldiers" and Ms. Cat is drinking a fresh lime and eating a Teen Burger.

ACT TWO

NARRATOR: It is the long awaited day. The day of the show down between Dilly and Ole Jack S. As the first rays of light streak the afternoon sky, Dilly, standing in the middle of the street looks at his watch, checks his gun, tightens his chaps and belches. Ms. Cat runs out and throws her arms around his neck and says

MS. CAT: Ya got a dime for a cup of Root Beer.

NARRATOR: Dilly replies, with dignity

DILLY: Oh yeah.

NARRATOR: Pestus and Doc enter arguing as usual.

DOC: Oh yeah.

PESTUS: Oh yeah.

DOC: Oh yeah.

PESTUS: Oh yeah.

DOC: Oh yeah.

PESTUS: Oh yeah.

NARRATOR: Miss Fifi runs out and screams

MISS FIFI: Here comes the judge.

NARRATOR: Enter Jack S., Pedro, Pancho and 120 bad guys.

JACK S: I'm going to draw my big .44's and shoot your head off.

PEDRO: Pancho Villa.

PANCHO: Si.

NARRATOR: Jack S. shouts

JACK S: I'm going to run over you with my wagon and step on your patent leather boots.

PEDRO: Ya Ta Hey.

PANCHO: Si.

NARRATOR: Jack S. resolves

JACK S: I'm going to mash you like a cockroach, kiss your woman, steal your horse and drink your Root Beer.

PEDRO: La Cucaracha

PANCHO: Si.

NARRATOR: Dilly responds majestically

DILLY: Oh yeah.

NARRATOR: Ms. Cat jumps in front of Dilly and screams

MS. CAT: I just washed his shirt and you better not get it dirty.

NARRATOR: Dilly bravely pushes her aside and says

DILLY: Oh yeah.

NARRATOR: Jack S., Pedro, Pancho and their men draw their guns and shoot 1352 times.

    (NO ONE FALLS)

Dilly draws his derringer and shoots one shot.

(EVERYONE ELSE FALLS)

As the story closes Matthew Dilly rides into the sunset singing the Male Quartet from the third act of the Barber Of Seville and law and order is restored to the West. The end.

(THE END)

Family Frolics, Relief Society Renditions and Sharing Time Skits -- Resource Manual

THE IGI CAPER
by
Charlee Cardon Wilson

CHARACTERS:
CHORUS -- 3-7 members
   (including Radio, Mommy, Policeman, Sheriff)
POP
JUNIOR

This skit may be done by a family or by a class to promote and explain in part some of the genealogical resources available, specifically, the IGI. Staging is simple. The chorus, is seated or standing to one side of the stage. Characters other than Pop and Junior may be members of the chorus and take their places as their turn comes. They then return to their chorus positions. The chorus uses choral reading techniques to provide back ground for the scene. This may be done as a reader's theatre or a memorized piece. The main characters especially Pop, must be absolutely dead-pan. The lines are spoken in a monotone, a la Jack Webb. Refer to old Dragnet episodes if possible. Costumes should be simple. Trench coats would be nice for Junior and Pop, but rain coats or over coats will do. Try to make Junior a carbon-copy of Pop costume-wise. Hats add a nice touch. Junior should mimic Pop's actions. Note pads and pencils are their only props. Two chairs are placed stage right. Chorus is stage left. Policeman needs large badge and police hat. Keystone cops style is great. Sheriff needs oversized cowboy hat and star. Use your imagination and have fun.

CHORUS: *(Dragnet theme)* Dum de dum dum. Dum de dum dum dah!
POP: This is the city, (name your city and state.)
JUNIOR: I live here.
POP: I'm his Pop. It was Monday, January l9th. 8:02 pm. It was quiet.
CHORUS: Too quiet!
POP: Family night was over.
CHORUS: Entirely too quiet.
POP: We were catching up some reports in the den.
CHORUS: Football scores.
POP: This is my partner, Junior. My name is Pop. We got a call.
RADIO: *(static is produced by paper being crumpled over a microphone, or chorus may chant static sounds. Announcer, a chorus member, holds nose and speaks)* APD *(Use your city's police department initials)* One and two, see the woman *(insert your address)* Code 516 742 110428...

(Announcer continues to read number until he is strangled by another chorus members)
CHORUS: Dum de dum dum. Dum de dum dum dah!
JUNIOR: Sounds serious.
POP: Missing persons report. Let's go.
CHORUS: Tramp, tramp, tramp, tramp
  (Repeat under next speech)
POP: We took the den exit to the hall, then headed east to the living room. We made good time.
  (Cross stage right to Mrs. Mommy)
CHORUS: *(faster)* Tramp, tramp, tramp, tramp
POP: *(Makes cut throat signal to chorus)* The woman's name was Mommy. She was obviously upset. She reported a missing relative, a woman.
MOMMY: All I know is, her name is Elizabeth.
  (She paces and wrings hands.)
POP: Do you have a description, Ma'am?
JUNIOR: A picture, maybe?
MOMMY: No, no, I don't I only know about her son, Jonathan. I've never met her personally.
POP: She has a son, Ma'am?
MOMMY: Why yes, she has several children.
JUNIOR: So, she's married, then?
MOMMY: Oh yes. Didn't I say that? Yes, she is.
POP: Would you know her husband's name, then?
MOMMY: Yes, here it is..uh...Mr. Lewis.
CHORUS: Dum de dum dum
  (Pop and Junior exchange knowing glances.)
JUNIOR: Would that be Ben Lewis, Ma'am?
MOMMY: Why yes, yes, how did you know?
CHORUS: Dum de dum..
  (Chorus is cut short by throat cutting gesture from Pop.)
JUNIOR: We were assigned to his case last month
MOMMY: His case?
POP: Missing parents, Ma'am.
CHORUS: Now?
POP: Now.
CHORUS: Dum de dum dum dah!
MOMMY: Did you find them?
JUNIOR: *(modestly)* We had good leads, Ma'am.
MOMMY: Oh, please, try to find Elizabeth too. It's so important that I locate her.
POP: We understand, Ma'am. We'll do our best.
MOMMY: Oh, I almost forgot. Here's all the information I have on her. There's

her marriage date, and here's where she was last time anyone saw her. Will this help?
JUNIOR: Yes, Ma'am, Thank you, Ma'am.
POP: We took the information Mrs. Mommy had given us and returned to headquarters.
JUNIOR: The den.
CHORUS: Tramp, tramp, tramp, tramp
> *(Mrs. Mommy returns to chorus as Pop and Jr cross slightly left of center stage, matching their footsteps to rhythm of chorus. Last two steps could be slightly syncopated or Junior and Pop could start to take a step and hesitate with one foot in the air trying to fake out the chorus. Chorus matches their "tramp" to Pop and Junior. This is a little tricky, but fun. Play with it.)*

POP: This is not one of your routine cases, Junior.
JUNIOR: How's that, Pop?
POP: Mrs. Elizabeth Lewis was last seen in Woburn, Massachusetts!
CHORUS: Dum de dum dum.
JUNIOR: And I just blew my allowance at the video arcade.
CHORUS: *(threateningly)* Dum de dum dum dah!
> *(Junior cowers and smiles sheepishly as Pop leans over him menacingly.)*

POP: One more thing.
CHORUS: Dum de dum dum
JUNIOR: Yeah, Pop, what's that?
POP: If this information is correct, Mrs. Lewis is approximately 270 years old.
CHORUS: Dum de dum duuuutch de dum duuutch etc.
> *(As a stuck record. Jr. walks over and pushes end chorus member who bumps the rest of the chorus.)*

Thanks, we needed that. Ahem! Dum de dum dum dah!
POP: Tuesday, January 20th, 10:03 AM. Junior and I headed downtown.
CHORUS: *(sound effects)* Brmmm, Brmmm, Brmmm, Brmmm,
> *(Motor noises, Junior and Pop sit on chairs stage right and vibrate or otherwise act out the sound effects. Pop is driving.)*

Beep, Beep
> *(Siren sound repeated two or three times)*

Screeech!
> *(Brake noise.)*

Cachunk!
> *(Car door)*

Walk, walk, walk, walk,
> *(Chorus member who is Policeman dons costume and walks forward, acts out sound effects.)*

Scribble, scribble, scribble, rrrripp
> *(Hands paper to Pop, who takes it with no expression)*

Walk, walk, walk, walk,
> *(Policeman returns to Chorus)*

Cachunk, Brmmm, Brmmm, Brmmm, Brmmm.
POP: Never honk at a black and white, son.
JUNIOR: I'll try to remember that, Pop. Where are we headed?
POP: We're going to check out the IGI.
JUNIOR: IGI?
POP: International Genealogical Index, alias, Computer File Index alias, Temple Bureau Index.
JUNIOR: This IGI must have some kind of record, Pop.
POP: Every record in the book, Junior. Christenings, baptisms, weddings, probate records...IGI has 'em all.
JUNIOR: Sounds like a pretty tough customer.
POP: You just have to remember one thing, Junior.
CHORUS: Dum de dum dum
JUNIOR: What's that, Pop?
POP: How to use a Microfiche Machine.
CHORUS: Dum de dum dum dah!
POP: 10:34 AM, we arrived at the branch library and went to the back room. It was dark.
CHORUS: Too dark!
POP: Junior tripped over a briefcase.
JUNIOR: Ouch!
CHORUS: Entirely too dark!
POP: No one looked up. They were desperate people. People hungry for information. People willing to try anything to satisfy their craving. They were into everything...parish registers, US census, four generation sheets. They'd try anything on film or fiche. Like I said, they were desperate. We finally connected with IGI sitting in the darkest corner. I could see this wasn't going to be easy. IGI never volunteers anything. We were going to have to pull it out the hard way. We started to work. 10:58 AM, we located North America. It was under M
JUNIOR: Pretty sneaky, huh, Pop.
CHORUS: M for North America.
(If your IGI is set up geographically or alphabetically, substitute appropriate descriptions.)
POP: IGI was determined to make our job difficult, but we had broken the code. The states were filed alphabetically.
JUNIOR: Pretty diabolical, huh, Pop.
CHORUS: *(alphabet song)* A,B,C,D,E,F,G
POP: We found Massachusetts under M.
CHORUS: Good deduction, Pop.
POP: The surnames were filed alphabetically too.
CHORUS: *(alphabet song continued)* H,I,J,K,L,M,N,O,P
POP: We were looking for Benjamin Lewis, the husband of Elizabeth.
CHORUS: Rewind!

(Alphabet song backwards)
P, O, N, M, L. L for Lewis.
POP: It was a long shot, but it paid off. The marriage was listed and the date agreed with the one Mrs. Mommy had given us. Elizabeth's maiden name was Jaquith. We decided to try another long shot. We checked Massachusetts for Jaquiths.
CHORUS: *(alphabet song backwards)* L, K, J. J for Jaquith.
POP: We found an Elizabeth Jaquith born June 1708 in Woburn the daughter of Abraham Jaquith and Sarah Jones. It looked pretty good. If she was our Elizabeth, then we had a line on her grandparents and great-grandparents too. We had to find out if she was the Elizabeth we were looking for. I sent Junior to order microfilm so we could find out where IGI got the information. We wanted to talk to the source. Meanwhile, I checked out the shelves in the library for early Massachusetts pioneers. I found a lead. If the Elizabeth Jaquith on the IGI was the right one, I'd discovered who she was and where she came from, plus her ancestry for several generations. Not bad for one day's work.
CHORUS: Way to go, Daddy, Smooth moves, Daddy
POP: Wednesday, January 1st, 4:30 PM..Junior and I checked the special collections branch of the public library. Junior found our subject. The pieces of the puzzle dropped into place like magic. We had traced the Jaquiths to their earliest American ancestry.
CHORUS: Dum de dum dum
POP: We also found a new clue...great grandfather Abraham was a Walloon.
CHORUS: Dum de dum dum what?
JUNIOR: What's a Walloon, Pop?
POP: Sounds like some kind of a bird, Junior.
JUNIOR: Abraham Jaquith was a bird, Pop?
POP: Sounds fishy to me, Junior.
JUNIOR: Me too, Pop, maybe we'd better investigate.
POP: Right, let's go.
   (Pop and Jr go to seats stage right and act out sound effects as before)
CHORUS: Brmmm, Brmmm, Brmmmm, Brmmm, beep, beep,
   (Siren sound 3 times)
  screech, cachunk, walk, walk, walk, walk,
    (Enter Sheriff)
  scribble, scribble, scribble, rrrip
    (Hands paper to Pop)
  walk, walk, walk, walk
    (Exit Sheriff)
  cachunk, brmmm, brmmm, brmmm, brmmm
POP: Never honk at a sheriff's vehicle either, Son
JUNIOR: I'll try to remember that, Pop.
ANNOUNCER: The subject, Elizabeth Jaquith, along with her parents,

grandparents and great grandparents were found related to Mrs. Mommy on January 26th, 1984. They were entered in Mrs. Mommy's genealogy on January 27th of the same year. Investigation into the Walloon ancestry of Abraham Jaquith is currently being conducted. The story you have just seen is semi-true. The names have been changed to protect the easily humiliated.

CHORUS: Dum-de-dum-dum-dum!

(THE END)

JONAH & THE BIG FISH
by
Sharon Elwell

Characters:
> **Jonah**
> Ship captain
> one crew member
> citizens of Nineveh
> Voice of the Lord

Props:

A cardboard box with the top and bottom cut out, big enough for Jonah, and the captain and crew to stand in.

A paper sail, made by poking holes through the top and bottom of a large piece of paper and putting a skewer through it'so it appears to billow, can be attached to the front of the ship.

Blue fabric can be stapled to the bottom of the ship, to hang to the floor and cover the legs Or the sailors.

A large sheet of cardboard, like a side of a washing machine box, with half-circles cut from one edge for the citizens of Nineveh to stand behind and rest their chins upon.

Cartoons of Ninevites are drawn on the cardboard. Remember, they were a surly bunch, and could be carrying signs such as "Jonah go home" "Down with Israel" "Nineveh, love it or leave it'" etc.

A big fish can be satisfactorily made by draping someone in black fabric and making a huge set of teeth to line their two arms. Egg cartons make very good teeth, and if your entire fish is not ferocious enough in appearance, he can lurk behind the drapes, then grab Jonah in his teeth at the appropriate moment, and drag him behind the curtains with him.

Scene One

Voice of the Lord: *(should be out of the room, and can read directly from scriptures)* Arise, go to Nineveh, that great city, and cry against it; for their wickedness is come up before me.
> *(Jonah stands up and begins packing and preparing to leave. Then he looks around for which way the voice came, and tiptoes off in the opposite direction.)*

Scene Two

Ship's Captain: Yes, I suppose we have room for one more. Where are you going?
Jonah: Wherever you are.
Captain: This ship is bound for Tarshish.
Jonah: That will be perfect. I've always wanted to see Tarshish.
> *(The storm can be produced by sound effects made on kitchen pots and pans in the next room, if you have the personnel. Or you can prepare the sound effects beforehand, experiment until they sound right, and tape record them to be turned on at this point. The Captain and Crew are praying loudly, and throwing imaginary things overboard. Jonah is sleeping.)*

Captain: Arise, sleeper, and call upon thy god, that we perish not.
Crew: Come, let us cast lots that we may know who has caused this evil to come upon us.
> *(Dice can be used here. Significant pause after throwing and looking.)*
> It's you! Tell us, what is your occupation? Where do you come from? Of what people are you?

Jonah: I am a Hebrew, and I fear the Lord, the God of Heaven, yet I fled from His presence. For this cause is this evil come upon you.
Captain: What shall we do unto thee, that the sea may be calm unto us?
Jonah: Take me up, and cast me forth into the sea, so the sea shall be calm unto you, for I know that for my sake this great tempest is upon you.
Captain: Maybe we can save you still. Let's row!
> *(They struggle, but grow weaker, and begin to pray.)*
> O God, let us not perish for this man's life, and lay not upon us innocent blood. He is in thy hands.
> *(They throw Jonah from the boat. He is immediately seized by the fish and dragged out of sight. The boatmen exit.)*

Jonah: *(His voice is heard praying)* Out of the belly of the earth I cry unto thee, and thou hast heard my voice. The billows and waves compassed me about even to the soul. The depths closed over me; the weeds were wrapped about my head. Yet thou hast saved my life, o Lord my God. My prayer came up unto thee. I will give what I have promised. Salvation is of the Lord.
> *(He falls out on the floor.)*

Voice of the Lord: (exactly as before) Arise. Go unto Nineveh, that great city and preach unto it the preaching that I bid thee.
> *(Jonah packs up, as before, but this time, he goes in the right direction.)*

Scene Three -- *People of Nineveh are looking and acting hostile as Jonah approaches.*

Jonah: You have only forty days until Nineveh shall be overthrown because of your iniquities.

People: *(Not together)* Oh, no! Forty days? Come, let us change our ways. Maybe if we repent and take heart, God will turn away His anger from us. Quickly! Let us find sackcloth and ashes. God has given us time! Let us not fail now!

> *(Jonah is horrified and angry. He sits down cross legged and pouts as the citizens leave in a hurry.)*

Jonah: *(very angry)* I pray thee now, Oh, Lord, take my life from me, for it is better for me to die than to live.

> *(Speaking almost to himself, at intervals)*

Why, what's this? A gourd plant growing up around me--and so rapidly! It's protecting me from the heat of the sun. Why, that's very nice! I feel much better! Now what? Oh, no! The plant is dying! It is withering away. Oh, now the sun is so hot again! Oh, I wish I could die. Without the shade, my life is miserable! Oh, Lord, take my life from me!

Voice of the Lord: Doest thou well to be angry for the gourd?

Jonah: I do well to be angry, even unto death!

Voice: Thou hast had pity on the gourd, for which you did not labor, nor madest it grow, which came up in a night and perished in a night. Should I not spare Nineveh, that great city, wherein are more than six score thousand persons?

(THE END)

Questions for Discussion:
1. How many are six score thousand persons?
2. Why do you think the Lord went to so much trouble to teach Jonah instead of choosing someone else?
3. Why do you think Jonah was angry instead of glad that the people repented and were saved?
4. How would you describe the personality of Jonah, based on what is recorded about him?
5. What do you think the Lord was trying to teach Jonah with the gourd?
6. Why was Jonah so reluctant to go to Nineveh?

LET FREEDOM RING
by Charlee Cardon Wilson

This presentation, suitable for Independence Day celebrations, picnics, breakfasts, etc., is also appropriate on other days of the year as a mutual lesson or Heritage Days skit. It may be done by a single class or a mixed group.

CHARACTERS
--1 youth or young adult
-- 5 girls (can be changed to boys or mixed, divided or combined to form any size group)

SMITH (Leader)
GAIL
MARY
SARAH
JANE
LIZ

NOTES:
Songs used in the presentation are available in choral arrangements at your local music store. If simpler arrangements are desired, most should be available at your local public library in folk song collections such as *The Weavers, Pete Seeger Song book,* or *Family Treasury of Folk Songs*. Choral arrangements of *O Freedom*, Ruth Artman, arranger, Hal Leonard, Publisher, and *This Land is Your Land*, Hal Leonard Publishing Co. are simple and effective. Other folk songs or patriotic songs may be substituted for those suggested. Use your local talent and resources. Most of these songs can be done with guitar accompaniment. If you're doing an outdoor production, consider taping accompaniment or using guitar and portable keyboards or other instruments.

[The scene is a classroom setting with a table center stage, a flag stands stage right or use two flags on either side of the stage. The girls are seated on both sides of the table facing the audience. The leader stands or moves across the stage as she speaks. She is holding a script in her hand]

SMITH: On this date, July 4, 1776, the Continental Congress met and announced to the world the ratification of the Declaration of Independence. Swaddled in her christening clothes, the Constitution, America came into being. The title of our presentation is "Let Freedom Ring". Freedom is the most important treasure an American has. It'should be cherished and protected like the rare jewel it is....

(She sighs and repeats to herself as she reads from the the script.)

...the rare jewel it is....oh brother!

(Addresses the audience)

I must tell all you adults in the audience that this script was written by the girls (youth), so you may find it a bit idealistic.

(The girls look at each other in alarm as the leader departs from the lesson. Each girl has a script in her hand which she consults as the leader seems to step out of character.)

I mean, it's a nice script, and has a lot of very good sentiments....but, it may come across just a little on the corny side to those of us who are older and wiser...

(Gail leaves seat and approaches leader, followed by other girls.)

GAIL: What do you mean by that, Sister Smith?

(Use real names of Reader and girls playing the parts.)

SMITH: Gee, I don't mean to rain on your parade or anything, but...well...right now, you guys get your whole concept of freedom from your American History teachers. I mean, that's okay. It's just that...well..it's just not a burning issue in today's world.

GIRLS: *(Ad lib)* What? Freedom is important! I don't believe you said that! What about other countries? etc.

SMITH: Shhh!

(Girls quiet gradually)

I'm not saying it isn't a great word, but nowadays, it's just that - a word.

(Girls begin to protest again)

Look, our forefathers fought for it. Generations have made laws to guarantee that it would never be lost. I mean, what's left to do? A little flag-waving and patriotic display once a year is nice, but face it - these days it's all show. Freedom is automatic for your generation.

GAIL: *(Grabs Sister Smith and sits her down on chair center sage.)*

Freedom isn't something handed out on a platter.

MARY: *(On Sister Smith's right. Smith looks up as each girl sings.)*

Freedom isn't something you can pick from a tree.

SARAH: *(Standing in back of chair, leans over to Sister Smith's left.)*

Freedom *(spoken)* Pay attention! It's a serious matter.

GIRLS:

You gotta work at freedom. It doesn't come free.

(Sister Smith tries to escape as girls sing chorus. Simple choreography is a nice addition.)

It's so! We know!
We'll pay the price for freedom
It's the way to go.
And we, can see

Freedom's up to you and me.

JANE: *(Sees Sister Smith trying to slip away stage right, grabs her and points stage left where Gail and Sarah pantomime a shoot-out.)*
Freedom is the prize that the patriots fought for.

LIZ: *(Leading Smith across stage, pointing right as Jane assumes Statue of Liberty pose.)*
Freedom is the beacon in America's hand.

SARAH: *(Takes Smith's arm as other girls link arms, putting Sister Smith in the middle for a chorus line kick.)*
Freedom is a hit, so let's call for an encore.

GIRLS:
If you love it, then don't lose it.
Come on take a stand.
It's so! We know!
We'll pay the price for freedom
It's the way to go.
And we can see
Freedom's up to you and me.

LIZ: *(A cheerleader type leads cheer. Choreography is in the drill team style. Words are chanted, not sung. Piano stops. Percussion may be used if desired.)* **Freedom of religion.**

JANE: Freedom of speech.
BOTH: Freedom to achieve the goals that stand in your reach.
SARAH: Freedom of expression.
GAIL: Freedom of the press.
MARY: Freedom to do nothing.
ALL: Freedom to progress.
F-R-E-E-D-O-M! Freedom! Freedom!! FREEDOM!!!
(Standard cheer ending.)

SMITH: *(Looking strained)* I rest my case. Freedom is a rah-rah word for patriotic rallies. It's a terrific thing for "team spirit". But, as a cause, it's passé.

JANE: *(Patronizing)* Sister Smith, let us simplify this. Let me tell you a story.
(Girls set up easel and large picture book. Sister Smith is escorted to a chair. Gail hands her a large teddy bear. Mary gives her a blanket. All girls get comfortable for story, some seated on the floor cross legged, one leaning on the back of Smith's chair or seated on the arm of the chair if there is one. Avoid having everyone seated in the same pose. One girl lays on her tummy, chin in hands. Jane must be a terrific storyteller. She needs to move around the stage and employ gestures and good eye contact with the audience as she tells the story. Book is a series of posters prepared by your local poster artist depicting the story as it's told. If Jane doesn't want to turn the pages, use one of the other girls. Book is optional.)

Once upon a time, in a make-believe place, there lived a young man and his new bride. These two good people set out to build a dream in the middle of a dense forest. Although the land was rocky and covered with thorns, they were determined to make the inhospitable place their home. Now this in itself was not remarkable, but as they fought back the wild beasts and cleared the land, they developed a curious practice of placing stones around the perimeter of their farm. These were not ordinary stones, though at first glance they may have seemed so. Underneath the dull gray algae that covered them, the stones were studded with a rare mineral that caught and reflected light. Even in the faintest moonlight, they glittered. The round stones were not easy to find. When located they required a brisk scrubbing to remove the clinging fungus which seemed to cover everything. Yet, despite the extra work involved, the couple patiently searched them out and polished them until they had a large farm bordered by the shining stones. Their work was far from finished. They plowed and planted weeded and harvested, and began to raise their family. In addition to all these chores, they continued to keep a vigilant watch on their sparkling border, here scrubbing away the ever encroaching algae, there replacing a stone that had been removed from it's place. This peculiar behavior did not go unnoticed by friends and relations. Soon, they were subjected to a good deal of kidding as well as some pointed criticism for their eccentricity. But the pair took the jibes in good humor, and as years passed and the farm prospered, the remarks died....For as strange as it'seems, the glittering border gave visitors a feeling of calm and safety. It'seemed to hold at bay the dark and forbidding forest. Indeed, the wild beasts wouldn't venture across the line of stones to prey upon the farm's livestock. Even the great predatory birds did not fly over the enclosed land to carry off the poultry or new lambs. The farm became a legend. People traveled from far and wide to marvel at its beauty. Some carried away a stone or two as souvenirs. The family found themselves spending more and more time searching out new stones to replace those that had been taken. Years passed swiftly. The children grew up and married. Grandchildren joined the family. More land was cleared. The stone borders were extended. The farm grew. It became habit with the large clan to gather in the evenings to discuss the day's business. At these happy meetings, the farmer and his wife would delight the grandchildren with tales of the early days on the farm. Because none of the little ones remembered the hardships of those times, the stories took on fairy-tale qualities. The tale related most often was the story of the search for the special border stones. It wasn't the most exciting story. In fact, many of the youngsters became quite bored the repetition, for they knew it by heart. Even more boring was the admonition which came at the end for all who lived on the farm to care for the stones. The younger generations found this task terribly tedious. They were eager to pursue more exciting things such as experimental crops and development of new farm equipment. Nevertheless, in deference to the old couple, the care of the stones continued, and the farm continued to thrive. Soon, it was known throughout the land for its innovative methods and blue ribbon livestock. It's famous stone border continued to sparkle, although the Patriarch's reminders to his children became more frequent and now and again, a scolding was required to get the job done. Then, the old couple passed on. Management of the farm was taken over by the children. Everyone was given a specialized job to do. Every task was assigned - except the care of the stones. This, it was decided, would continue to be a community responsibility. In truth, very little importance was placed on the maintenance of the border. It was considered by most to be an old-fashioned idea, and while they thought it quaint, it required too much time to properly maintain. The borders nearest the cottages were given half-hearted attention, but no one assumed the responsibility for the stones at the far edges of the fields. Soon, creeping lichen covered long sections of the border. Wild animals, no longer shied away from the stones. The beasts began hunting on the furthest pastures. The farm lost its first livestock. Predators quickly became such a threat that no one wanted to work the far fields. They were abandoned. The tangled forest growth swiftly reclaimed the land. As the forest advanced, so did the wild beasts. More stock was lost; more land was given back to the wilderness. There was no more room for experimental crops. There were no funds to support development of new equipment and methods. The family began to quarrel among themselves. Each one blamed someone else for the farm's decline. One brave young man spoke up and called for a community effort to clean and replace the border stones. He was greeted with jeers. Everyone was much too busy with his own tasks to go out and polish rocks! The farm deteriorated. Most of the family left, giving up ownership to work in less hostile surroundings. Those that remained lived in destitute circumstances. There was little to eat and much to fear from the dark wilderness that once again surrounded them. One day, a girl, looking for grass to feed her scrawny sheep, found several round, algae-covered stones. As she rubbed away the crumbly growth, she saw a sparkle. "What a pretty garden border these would make," she said to herself. "If I look for one new stone each day...."

GAIL: *(Jumping up)* You see, the stones represent freedom.
LIZ: Yeah! And the algae is...like...apathy, you know, no one cares....
SARAH: Uh-huh, and this algae, or apathy is constantly creeping forward
   (She creeps forward menacingly)
to dull our freedom.
MARY: *(Becoming oratorical)* You see, everybody has to work at keeping our freedom polished. We must keep the corner stone of the nation sparkling. Ask not what your country can do for you. Ask what you can do....
   (Sister Smith places her hand over the orator's mouth.)
SMITH: Yes, well, that's the whole problem. We're too big! I can't do it all. What good does it do for me to be concerned about freedom? I can't scrub off everyone else's algae..uh, apathy too.

GAIL: *(Condescendingly)* You weren't listening to the end of the story. Remember the girl who found a few of the stones? She didn't want to try and put a border around the whole farm - just her little corner of it.
JANE: Yeah, and she was gonna work at it one stone at a time.
SMITH: Fine, I have the freedom to decide what color to paint my bathroom. What I'm saying is...freedom doesn't mean as much today as it did in the old days.
SARAH: Look, if you really want to know what freedom means, ask someone who's been denied it.
MARY: She means like slaves. The only freedom from slavery for them was death.

(music fades in. Song: Oh, Freedom!)

SMITH: Okay so that's a good example. The constitution gave all men the right to life, liberty and the pursuit of happiness. But just look at how it was denied to some.
LIZ: Gotta polish those rocks, Sister Smith.
> *(Sets rock on table, shines it with a cloth. Rock is sprayed gold or silver. Letters spelling out "freedom" are painted in red, white and blue on the side away from the audience.)*

Everybody's gotta polish those rocks.
GAIL: Yeah, and sometimes, it's not too easy to do. We had to fight a war to end slavery.
JANE: The Civil War! What a sad time that was...families divided against one another.

(Fade in background music: Dixie or Battle Hymn)

The North won. But in a Civil war, everyone loses.
MARY: Ask the wives and mothers of those who didn't come home.

(Music changes to Rally Round the Flag played as a dirge.

> *(Girls sing quietly in background as Sarah recites and dramatizes poem.)*

SARAH: *(Places shawl on her head, walks slowly across the stage, carrying a flower in her hand, kneels as if at a grave.)*
Our dreams are shattered pieces
Crushed 'neath the wheels of war.
Am I a fool to question
What was your dyin' for?
Do you suppose it mattered?
Would anyone have cared?
Oh Johnny, I'm so selfish.

I'm all alone...and scared.
There must be others like me
Left behind to mourn,
Vainly mending tatters
Of lives so badly torn.
I guess it makes no difference now
The color that they wore:
Just someone's sweetheart, someone's son
Won't come home any more.
Oh Johnny!
To them you were just a toy soldier
To be won or lost in little boy's game.
They don't think of soldiers as somebody's children,
Somebody's fathers, with faces and names.
Johnny, you're here, and I count myself lucky.
For so many kinsmen, stalwart and brave
Lie 'neath some battlefield, lost and forgotten
With no tree to shade them, no stone for their grave.
Time heals all wounds, Love,
So everyone tells me.
I'll pick up the pieces.
I'll make my own way.
I'll be living tribute to all that you fought for
Until I can slumber beside you someday.
'Til then, my love, farewell.

(She rises, as girls sing chorus once through, she crosses back and removes shawl.)

SMITH: You guys argue a good case. Okay, I agree, I guess some freedoms don't come easy. But, what about freedom of religion. No one took up arms to insure our pioneer ancestors got to worship as they chose. They were chased across half the nation.

LIZ: Yeah, but they polished those rocks, Sister Smith. Ya gotta keep polishing those rocks.

(She polishes rock and places it on table.)

ALL: Come, Come Ye Saints

*(Audience may be invited to sing along on **Come, Come Ye Saints**.)*

SMITH: Well, I guess what frustrates me is that even today our constitutionally guaranteed freedoms are being abused. I know our forefathers never intended their words to give some slimy character the right to peddle pornography or pollute our public air waves.

GIRLS: Ya gotta polish those rocks, Sister Smith!

(Place rock on table.)

MARY: That's what we've been trying to tell you. It's your responsibility.
JANE: Yeah, if you see dirty magazines on display in a store where you shop, use your freedom of speech. Tell them you won't shop there until they get rid of the nasty things.
    (Place rock on table.)
MARY: Write a letter to the editor. circulate a petition. Crush the wild beasts of perversion who are preying on our land from the mountains, to the valleys, to the oceans white with foam....
    (Realizes she's been carried away again.)
....uh....God bless America!
    (Places rock on table.)
GAIL: (Sighing and shaking her head) Well, what she's trying to say, Sister Smith, is that this isn't just my country or their
    (Indicate audience)
...country. This land is your land too.
SMITH: *(Groans)* Oh, what a sneaky way to get in another song.
    (She joins girls and invites audience to sing along)

This Land is Your Land

SMITH: Okay, I'm sold. Where do I start?
    (Girls lean forward as if to tell her)
Oops...I know...I gotta keep polishing those rocks.
    (Places rock on table.)
Okay, give me some ideas. Which rock do I start with?
LIZ: Be aware of community events. Take part in neighborhood activities.
SMITH: I can polish that rock.
    (Turns first rock around so that letter is visible to the audience.)
SARAH: Be an aid at your children's school.
SMITH: I can polish that rock.
    (Turns second rock.)
GAIL: Read the newspaper, and not just Dear Abby.
SMITH: Hey, that one I do already! I can definitely polish that rock.
    (Turn third rock.)
SARAH: Read up on the issues and vote!
SMITH: I can polish that rock.
    (Turn fourth rock.)
MARY: Write your congressman.
SMITH: There's a thing or two I'd like to tell him. I can polish that rock.
    (Turn fifth rock.)
JANE: Fast and pray for the leaders of our nation.
SMITH: We can all polish that rock!
    (Turn sixth rock.)
MARY: Teach your children; teach us how to polish our own freedom stones. If

we learn while we're young, we'll be better citizens.
SMITH: We can help each other on that one. We can all polish that rock.
 (Turn last rock)
Looks like we're gonna have a lot of shiny stones laying around.
GAIL: Nope. What we're gonna have is freedom.

[Music lead in]

LIZ:
Freedom of religion.
MARY:
Freedom of speech.
SMITH:
Freedom to achieve the goals that stand in your reach.
JANE:
Freedom of expression.
GAIL:
Freedom of the press.
SARAH:
Freedom to do nothing.
ALL:
Freedom to progress.
Freedom must be tended like a seed that is planted. Irrigate with brotherhood. Weed out bigotry. Cultivate it daily. Never take it for granted. And soon you'll be a-sittin' 'neath a liberty tree.
Freedom!
You spell that liberty
Freedom!
It's elementary that
Freedom!
Depends on you and me.
So sing out Freedom's melody.
 (Repeat last chorus ending with:)
So don't sit idly lookin'
Come on girl (folks) get cookin'
Sing out Freedom's melody.
(Shout) Freedom!

(THE END)

Family Frolics, Relief Society Renditions and Sharing Time Skits -- Resource Manual

MALADIES PECULIAR TO THE MORMON FAITH
By Charlee Cardon Wilson

CHARACTERS: (only five speaking roles)
Master of Ceremonies
5 Medical Students
2 Orderlies (non-speaking)
Sketch 1: VICTIM: Mother. PANTOMIMISTS: Mother, Father, 2 Teen sons, pre-teen son
Sketch 2: VICTIM: Sister Teacher. PANTOMIMISTS: Teacher, 10 children
Sketch 3 -- VICTIM: Woman. PANTOMIMISTS: 3 women
Sketch 4 -- VICTIM: Child on crutches. PANTOMIMISTS: Small Child, Older Sibling, Father, Mother.
Sketch 5 -- VICTIM: Mother. PANTOMIMISTS: Mother, Teen.

NOTE: This skit also works well with slides rather than actors. The youth seem to enjoy preparing the scenes and getting each shot just right. It makes a nice Parent Appreciation presentation.

This skit may be done in a variety ways. Each case may be presented by a different "medical student", or all may be presented by a single narrator. If the medical student approach is used, the speakers should be dressed in white coats and stand on the floor with the "victim" seated pathetically by their side. The victim may show an occasional symptom if appropriate. The stage is where the action takes place with each scene acted out as described. All action is "freeze frame" where actors change and hold poses as directed. Use an introduction appropriate to the occasion for which the skit is performed. If medical students are used, the Master of Ceremonies may wish to introduce each one with the Malady they will be talking about. Each lecturer may put the facts into his own words or read from his "notes" and do it as written.

MASTER OF CEREMONIES: MONDAY MOLLY GRUBS
(Enter "victim" escorted by white coated orderlies who stand behind her chair while presentation is being made.)
STUDENT: Cause: Family Home Evening conflict with Monday night foot ball.
(Family Scene is lit on stage. Mother standing back to audience. Television, also back audience is to her left. Male family members are facing her and looking bored, worried, angry, etc. Use whatever ages and expressions you wish.)
Symptoms: Usually occur in the male members of the family and most often is most severe in the adolescent male, especially if it is his turn to give the

lesson.
> *(Change poses to reflect the progress of the disease. One boy could be on knees pleading, one stands by set gesturing with one hand toward it, etc. Use your imagination.)*

First signs are a general sulkiness with shuddering sighs and an occasional whimper followed by longing looks at the TV set and frequent checking of the time.
> *(Change poses again.)*

Conversation will run the gamut from long, passionate oratory on the teams playing and the importance of the game to surly monosyllabic replies to questions.
> *(Stage goes dark or curtain closes.)*

Treatment: Two aspirin for the wife and mother who must endure to the end of the arguments. Compromise with either a short, quick lesson during half time, or change family night to a non-football evening. Neither treatment is totally satisfactory but research is continuing and the syndrome usually becomes less acute during the winter months when it is replaced by Monday Night Basketball Blues.
> *(Victim is helped off by the orderlies. If several medical students are used, the next one is introduced.)*

MASTER OF CEREMONIES: POST PRIMARY PROSTRATION
> *(Enter victim escorted by orderlies, or carried in on a stretcher if desired. Stage has primary scene.)*

STUDENT: Cause: 1) Having ten children show up on the day you prepared six treats.
> *(Frantic teacher, her back to children is holding roll in one hand and treat box in the other.)*

2) Discovering that the sweet little boy who cuddled up on your lap and said he wasn't ever going to miss Primary even if he got mumps and chicken "pops" has both and you've never had either.
> *(Teacher is seated with small boy on her lap reading from a large picture book to class.)*

3) Rehearsing for the Sacrament Meeting Presentation on the day that three classes spent the entire pre-primary period seeing who could drink the most water fastest. Complication: The plumbing in the nearest rest room is out of order.
> *(Teacher is bending over while child whispers in her ear. Line of children stands behind the whisperer in various poses that suggest discomfort. One child is frozen in a quick walk position heading out the door. After causes are read, stage goes dark.)*

Symptoms: General aching, possibly acute pain in the head, neck and legs. Extreme fatigue may be present. In extreme cases, hysteria, incoherent babbling or nervous tics may be brought on by placing any child under twelve in the same room with the patient.

(He demonstrates, motions a child toward him. The victim, demonstrates all three symptoms and runs screaming from the room followed by the orderlies.)

Treatment: Two aspirin for pain, a quiet bedroom for fatigue, and Kentucky Fried Chicken for dinner. Experimental cases wherein pregnancy is used to cure the disease by removing the patient from the source of the illness has proved at best to achieve only brief remissions.

MASTER OF CEREMONIES: THE SUNDAY MULTI-MEETING MALADY

(Enter victim in wheelchair pushed by orderlies)

STUDENT: Cause: Continuous marathon-style meetings from early morning until late evening. Most prevalent on Correlation Council and Mutual Presidency Meeting Sundays.

(Lights up on stage where three women are seated on a bench. One holds child [[doll] and is craftily stealing a bite of baby food from a jar.)

Symptoms: 1) Blurred vision, add stomach, and light headedness from missed meals. These are sometimes replaced by indigestion and a grouchy baby when one tries in desperation to alleviate ones hunger by pilfering the infants strained spinach and bananas. In this case, a severe guilt complex will also become manifest.

(Poses change. Second woman is now standing, profile to the audience. She is wearing a box under her skirt which gives her a square bottom.)

2) Pew Posterior or Bench Bottom results when ones hind quarters begin to mold themselves to the contours of the bench or chairs, causing extreme discomfort and ill--fitting clothing.

(Change pose. Third woman is now standing and looking down at her legs where her panty hose have crept down around her shins. She has a slip bunched below her bosom. There is a line midway around her hips where her girdle has rolled down. First and Second women hold previous poses)

3) Creeping underwear caused by girdling ones loins in an eighteen-hour girdle for nineteen or more hours. In acute cases, the top of the girdle rolls down cutting off circulation to the lower body while the panty hose slip down even further shackling one's ankles together. The slip bunches up just below bra line creating a second, and in some cases, conspicuously larger bosom.

(Stage goes dark.)

Treatment: Carry dehydrated foods to nibble surreptitiously during meetings. Caution should be exercised as tragic incidents have resulted when dehydrated food nibblers have tried to drink water between meetings. This practice causes extreme swelling. Some cases have been reported where patients became so engorged that they became wedged in hallways. No satisfactory treatment of pew posterior is available at this time. However, the clothing industry is aware of the problem and are designing new styles which they hope will get to the seat of the matter. Creeping underwear is also

virtually unresearched. Relief at this time may only be obtained by leaving the bothersome underwear at home and letting it all hang out.
(Orderlies escort patient off.)

MASTER OF CEREMONIES: THE ONE SHOE-TWO FEET SYNDROME
(Enter a child on crutches)
STUDENT: Cause: Burglars, malidous ghosts, cockroaches, family pets or siblings, but never, never the fault of the victim.
(Lights up on stage. Small child holding one shoe is crying. Father is yelling, Mother is searching room. Older sibling is giving younger one dirty look.)
Symptoms: Occurs on Sunday mornings or fifteen minutes before major Ward activities. Attacks children mainly but cases in the adult and adolescent age brackets are not unknown. First symptoms are anger, frustration, and/or tears. This is accompanied by an announcement that there is a shoe missing, stolen, or devoured that was there just a few minutes ago
(Change poses. Older child and Younger child are now fighting openly. Mother is still searching. Father is trying to referee the fight.)
This is followed by accusations by the victim, counter accusations by the accused, complete recounting of past misdeeds, deteriorating into an exchange of snide personal remarks.
(Change pose and add another older child to fight, Mother still searching. Father looking at his watch and pointing to the door.)
During the first stage and continuing through the final stages, Father makes periodic announcements of the precise time. This increases in volume and intensity as the meeting time draws nearer. Acute cases include a real countdown with hysteria and possible physical injury to the loser and alleged losee.
(Stage goes dark.)
Treatment: Two aspirin for Mother's headache, an organized family search of the premises if time permits. Alternate plans permit the semi-barefoot child to wear this tennis shoes provided neither of those are missing also. As a last resort, bandage the unshod foot, hand the kid a crutch and order him to limp. It is not advisable to force a younger brother to wear his older sister's shoes as this subjects him to ridicule by his peers.
(Exit child)

MASTER OF CEREMONIES: THE RELIEF SOCIETY EAR
(Enter woman with bandaged head and dazed look. She is seated by orderlies. She is in an almost catatonic state, head held to one side.)
STUDENT: Cause: Position of responsibility in any organization complicated by a telephone in the home. Condition is most severe in presidencies of auxiliaries
(Stage lights come up. Woman is posed with telephone resting on shoulder.

She is preparing dinner.)
Symptoms: Begins with slight reddening of the ear accompanied by tenderness and swelling. The condition progresses to blistering of the ear tissue and eventually, open sores

(Change pose. Woman is now gesturing with hands to teen who is asking her a question.)

In later stages, patient begins using only hand signals to communicate with persons present in the room.

(Change pose. Woman has become hunchbacked, a maniacal gleam in her eye, index finger extended.)

Deformity results from clamping the receiver between head and shoulder. The index finger becomes fixed in a rigid dialing or push button position. Finally the patient will not respond vocally to any conversation not preceded by the ringing of a telephone bell.

(Stage Dark)

Treatment: Only two rather drastic measures have ever proven effective in this condition. A temporary stop-gap which does not prevent future flare-ups is pregnancy. This usually insures release from the position for a brief time and allows the ear to heal. Side effects of this treatment are nausea, abdominal swelling, and in some cases, offspring younger than the patients grandchildren. The second, more permanent method is complete amputation of the phone and phone lines from the house. This results in immediate enforced withdrawal from outside society. It may also trigger psychotic behavior which will compel the patient to rush to public phone booths and deposit coin after coin just to hear the dial tone. Patients have been known to snatch ringing business phones from the hands of secretaries insisting, "It's for me!" The sight of a switchboard can send the patient into a catatonic state.

(Phone rings, patient jumps up, yells:

PATIENT: It's for me!

(PATIENT runs off chased by orderlies and medical student.)

MASTER OF CEREMONIES: Other Mormon Maladies to covered at a later date will include: Building Fund Billfold, Roadshow Rash Dress Standard Doldrums, Visiting Teacher's Virus, and Nursery Leader Knees. Please plan to join us then.

(THE END)

NEPHI AND LABAN
by Sharon Elwell

Characters:
Nephi
Angel
Zoram
Laman
Lemuel
Voice (representing the Holy Ghost)
Sam
Laban
Servants (non-speaking parts; good for small children)
> *(If your group is small, combine Laman and Lemuel into one character, use the same person for the angel and the voice, and let Zoram represent all the various servants. Or invite another family over to do this with you so that you'll have some people left over to take pictures, pop popcorn, and applaud.)*

Props: treasure chest with coins and jewelry, Laban's sword, brass plates, Laban's helmet and armor

Scene One -- *Nephi and his brothers are seated on the floor in Laban's house; the treasure chest is open on the floor in front of them. Laban is seated on a chair. Servants, including Zoram, stand at his side.)*

Laman: So you see, Uncle, we have brought all our precious things for you. You are welcome to everything we have. All we ask is that the records of our fathers that are on the plates of brass go with us on our journey.

Laban: You have a great treasure here. Let me see.
> *(He examines the treasure.)*

Lemuel: All the treasures of my father's house will be yours.

Laban: *(chuckles)* Yes, they will. Indeed, they will. Zoram, carry these things into the treasury.
> (Zoram exits with chest.)

Laman: Are the brass plates in the treasury, Uncle?

Laban: Yes. And that is where they will stay!
> *(Standing, he shouts)*

Get out of my house, foolish nephews. And never return, if you value your lives! Call the guards! After them! And if you catch them, slay them!
> *(The boys flee. Laban is left alone, laughing wickedly.)*

Scene Two -- *The four brothers are huddled together in a cave.*

Laman: I don't see the torches any longer. They must have given up the chase.
Sam: Thank goodness! Then we are safe for a moment.
Lemuel: Safe? We will never be safe. If we return to Jerusalem, Laban will have us killed, and if we go to our father in the wilderness, he will punish us for failing to bring the plates!
Laman: He's right. What do you say now, Nephi? You told us that God would not send upon this errand without making it possible for us to accomplish it. You almost got us killed. You're just like Father. Once you get a foolish idea in your head, you never stop.
Nephi: I still say that the Lord will help us to obey our father.
Lemuel: I don't know about you, but I'm through trying to obey our father. I'm not going back into that desert.
Laman: Neither am I. I don't intend to dry up out in that endless wasteland.
Nephi: But the Lord has commanded us. . .
Laman & Lemuel: Yes? Well, where's he hiding now? I've heard enough out of you...look where you've got us...
   (They pick up sticks and begin hitting Nephi. The angel appears.)
Angel: Why do ye smite your younger brother with a rod? Know ye not that the Lord hath chosen him to be a ruler over you and this because of your iniquities? Behold, ye shall go up to Jerusalem again, and the Lord will deliver Laban into your hands.
   (Angel exits.)
Laman: Deliver Laban into our hands? How would it be possible?
Lemuel: He has fifty men at his command; he could slay fifty Why not us?
Nephi: Let us go again unto Jerusalem, and let us be faithful in keeping the commandments of the Lord, for behold, he is mightier than all the earth, then why not mightier than Laban and his fifty--yes or even his tens of thousands?
Sam: Nephi is right; the Lord is able to deliver us. Let us go back.
Nephi: Let us be strong like unto Moses, for he truly spake unto the waters of the Red Sea and they divided hither and thither and our fathers came through, out of captivity, on dry ground, and the armies of Pharaoh did follow and were drowned in the waters of the Red Sea.
Sam: Now behold, we know that this is true.
Nephi: Ye also know that an angel hath spoken unto you; wherefore can ye doubt? Let us go. The Lord is able to deliver us, even as our fathers, and to destroy Laban, even as the Egyptians.
   (Exeunt.)

Scene Three -- *Nephi enters a dark street in Jerusalem. He is alone. Laban is unconscious at the far end of the street.)*

Nephi: Oh, Father, I wish my brothers had come with me into the city. Guide me to accomplish this task, for I know not what to do, nor which way I should go.
   (Sees Laban.)
   What's this? A drunken man? Oh, no! It's my uncle
   (Draws Laban's sword from its sheath.)
   How beautiful this sword is. Pure gold--and precious steel for the blade. I've never seen one like it.
Voice: Slay him.
Nephi: Oh, no. Never at any time have I shed the blood of man. I cannot.
Voice: Behold, the Lord hath delivered him into thy hand.
Nephi: That is true...and I know that he sought to take away my own life. Neither does he keep the Lord's commandments, and surely he has stolen our property. But I cannot!
Voice: Slay him, for the Lord hath delivered him into thy hands. Behold, the Lord slayeth the wicked to bring to pass His righteous purposes. It is better that one man should perish than that a nation should dwindle and perish in unbelief.
Nephi: Yes, I remember the Lord's words that if our seed would keep the commandments they will prosper in the land of promise to which we go. And surely they cannot keep the commandments if they do not have them. And the law that was given to Moses is on the plates of brass. We must have the record!
   (Lifting Laban by the hair, he cuts off his head, then swiftly takes Laban's helmet and armor and dresses himself.)

<u>Scene Four</u> -- *Outside Laban's house. Nephi, disguised as Laban, sees Zoram passing the door and recognizes him as the servant who took the jewels to the treasury.)*

Nephi: *(disguising his voice)* Ho! You there! Go with me now into the treasury.
Zoram: Yes, Master. How did you find the elders at the meeting, Sir? Was the business soon concluded?
Nephi: Were it'soon concluded, I would be already asleep. No, the elders never conclude quickly. Foolish men, speaking on and on about nothing...I need the engraved plates of brass. I must carry these to my brethren. And come thou with me.
Zoram: Yes, sir. I shall carry these heavy plates. Tell me, was Brother Ishmael recovered? Was he present at the meeting?
Nephi: Uh...no. He was not there.
Zoram: A pity. The poor man. It was truly dreadful business, was it not, sir?
Nephi: Dreadful. Well, yes, I say so. Hurry, can't you? The brethren await us .

We don't need all this conversation.

Scene Five -- *Outside the city. The three brothers are crouched behind a rock, waiting.)*

Laman: Oh, no! Here comes Laban. He's killed our brother, and now comes for us!
Lemuel: He doesn't see us yet. Let's run for our lives!
   (They jump up and begin to run.)
Nephi: (shouting) Wait!
   (They recognize his voice and stop.)
Zoram: *(terrified)* Oh, no! What have I done?
   (He turns to run, but Nephi overpowers him.)
Nephi: *(holding the struggling Zoram)* Listen! Now, if you will only listen, as the Lord liveth and as I live, we will spare your life!
   (Zoram stops struggling)
You need not fear. On my oath, if you will come with u, you shall be a free man. The Lord hath commanded us to do this, and surely we must. You shall have place with us if you will.
Zoram: If these things be true, then I will go with you. And I will remain with you hence forward.
Sam: It is well. Now no one will know of our flight and there will be none to pursue and destroy us.
Laman: We have tarried here too long already. Let the foolish business be concluded. Let's begin our journey at once.
Nephi: Yea.- Jerusalem, that great city, holds nothing for us now. Our parents surely grow weary with waiting. A great destiny is before us. To the wilderness!
All: To the wilderness!

(THE END)

Discussion Questions
1. Why do you think Laban didn't want to give up the plates?
2. Is there another instance in scripture where a person has been instructed by the Lord to break a commandment?
3. How do you think Nephi was able to tell that the instruction came from God?
4. What do you think would have happened if they had left for this continent without the brass plates?
5. What was on the brass plates that was so important?

THE NO-TALENT
by
Charlee Cardon Wilson

This skit is done as a monologue. The setting may be either a living room with a rocker, end table, lamp and rug, or it may be a kitchen setting with a cabinet (or table) and telephone. If the living room setting is chosen, the sister is seated in the rocker knitting or crocheting. There is a cardboard box on the floor by the side of the rocker. It is open, and the flaps prevent the audience from seeing what is written on the outside of the box. The sister carries on the monologue as if the audience were a close friend visiting in her home. This setting is ideal for an older sister. If the kitchen setting is used, the conversation may be carried on over the telephone, or as if the audience is visiting with the sister in the kitchen She is wiping off the outside of a number of jars of canned fruit or jam as she talks. She is also labeling them and putting them into two cardboard boxes. The flaps on the boxes prevent the audience from seeing what is written on the outside. If the telephone is used, it'should have a long cord and a shoulder rest.

SISTER: I hadn't wanted to go to begin with. Those affairs always depress me so - all those talented, creative women I always come home feeling like such a dolt...the original mediocre Mary. But, then I thought of poor Ellen with her foot in that clumsy old cast, and recalled how depressed she'd sounded on the phone Boy, did she ever have a case of cabin fever.
    (Laughs)
Do you remember that feeling? I sure do!
    (A young sister may say: I can certainly identify with that feeling!)
Anyhow, I figured maybe if I went and invited her to ride along, she'd feel better. Sure enough, when I asked her, she'd just been dying to go. Course, you know her and she'd never call up and ask for a ride right up front. So, that's how I got myself committed. Then I though, as long as I had to be there, I'd just as well take a whole car-load. So, I called up Jill and Betty and Old sister Carmody and her sister, and that new girl with all the little kids that just moved in. Course, being new, she didn't have a sitter, nor knew anyone to ask, so I picked up June's oldest daughter on my way back from visiting & Sister Weaver....You remember her the rest home. Well, I drop by there every other day or so to knit and rock She does the most beautiful Afghans you've ever seen I took a couple by the knitter's Nook and they sold right of. Thrilled Sister Weaver to death to earn a little pin money Now she knits so much, I have a hard time keeping her in yarn. Come with me next time I go see her. She's a real card!

Well, as I was saying, I got everyone rounded up and went. I'd made up my mind not to come home feeling bad. Naturally, once I got there, I was glad I'd gone It was spectacular! You can't imagine the displays! I've never seen the like... Let's see, Genevieve had several of her paintings hung

Gorgeous things! I don't know how she finds the time with all those children! Remember when her four oldest were small and she was carrying the twins? You recall..Doc put her right down in bed for six weeks Nobody knew how she was going to manage. And Bob was no help at all, what with working days and getting his degree nights. Well, of course, you do what you have to. She still says it was the longest six weeks she's ever spent. Well, anyway, I was over there helping out week days and she decided to paint some Easter outfits for those little kids She was feeling pretty restless, you know. Well, all she had was a few yards of unbleached muslin..or was it kettle cloth?..oh well, whatever it was, it was awful plain. But, I managed to get three simple little dresses and a vest and short pants out of it Nothing fancy at all until she used her textile paints. That was all she had then - textile paints She painted up those ugly little things 'til they looked fit for royalty. Well, Easter Sunday, I just had to stop by and tell her what a stir her little ones caused at church. Bob was just bustin', he was so proud I took that old brownie camera of mine and snapped a picture of those kids out front of the church.took it to her in the hospital later. She's got it in a fancy frame on the mantel up at the new house.

Oh.well, I do get side-tracked Let's see...who else... Oh Adelle Stevenson sang something from some opera. I couldn't understand a word - it was one of those foreign ones, but I just had goose bumps all over. Couldn't help smile when I remembered that that pretty, poised young woman was the same pudgy seventeen-year-old with braces who used to come by. She'd be there every week or so taking up my whole afternoon crying about some crisis or other. And it was no good trying to work while she talked. She wanted full and undivided attention. Bless her heart. Sometimes I thought she was gonna stay right through the millennium. Oh yes, I tell you, I was tempted to duck down and pretend I wasn't home occasionally, but my conscience never'd let me. After all, what does listening cost anybody? The housework will always be there tomorrow. Like I said, I couldn't help but smile.
Ruby Jones played a violin solo. When I compare her playing to my grandson's, I can hardly believe they're the same instrument

(Young woman may substitute nephew or son)

Remember the spring we went over and helped Ruby plant her garden'? Never saw anybody so thrilled by a new radish in all my life! She came over at a dead run the morning she found it I had to drop everything and go see the miracle. I didn't have the heart to tell her it was a tumbleweed. It didn't matter, though, the next day the whole row was up and I just ripped her pride and joy out when she wasn't looking...Now don't you tell. Oh, just everybody was there - Sister Keeler with her ceramics couple of the vases I recognized from that night when young John was taken to the hospital with his appendix. She had some pieces in the kiln. I was just off my volunteer shift, so she sent me back to get 'em out before they were ruined. ever had the slightest idea what I was doing, but they must've come out all right. Real pretty - bright blue with pink roses.

- Let's see, Margo played the piano. Something real fast. It'sounded hard -- just like on television, but she didn't use the music. She played for Adelle too Then some sisters I didn't know from up North sang a madrigal. Oh, and Sister Peterson read some of her poetry. I hadn't seen her since our last envelope stuffing project last year. You may not know her. She was never even active until I started dragging her out to work parties. Why she preferred them to regular meetings, I'll never figure out. Anyway, it broke the ice, I guess She told me she's canning chairman in her new ward. She loves it! You watch; she'll have that ward triple their production and we'll all be expected to keep up. She's a real work horse...and her poetry...Oh my! She takes everyday words and puts them together and they come out sounding elegant She can make you laugh or cry Somebody told me she's gonna get some things published. I hope so. I told her I'd always wanted to know somebody famous.
- I must confess I enjoyed myself. Met so many old friends. It's a pity we don't see each more often. You know how it is though, everyone's busy, and now that the Stake has been divided, there're just so few opportunities I had a lot of nice visits; brought back a lot of special memories. The others seemed to have a good time too,..especially Ellen. I practically had to drag her away. We almost closed up the building. We stopped off for ice cream on the way home. You know how much Sister Carmody relishes strawberry, her sister too. Just like a couple of little kids. I didn't come home feeling sorry for myself either. You know, I thought about it a lot and I figure the Lord made some folks plain and others fancy, and I guess it takes one to appreciate the other. Heaven knows I'm of the plain variety I can't sing anything but lullabies and finger painting is the only art I can manage Actually, my finger painting wouldn't stand up against a three-year-old's. But, the grand kids say I draw the best kitties in church. Guess that'll be my claim to fame

    (Laughs)
- Even my needlework is more functional then decorative. There! one!

    (She folds knitting, lifts box takes inventory as she talks The flap is now up so that the audience can see that the box is labeled "Elders mending and Winter Wear")
- Poor Elder B has been waiting on this box for two weeks now. Get your coat and ride along to deliver it, why don't you.

    (She rises, closes box with tape.)
- Yup, I decided my talent must be being a good audience. So I'm going to make sure I develop it by encouraging those with fancier talents. Guess that makes me coming to those kind of shows kinda important too....

(Wistfully)
Still, it must be a satisfying thing to do something that touches so many people like some folks do. You know what I mean?
(She exits.)

(THE END)

For kitchen Scene, substitute: Even my cooking is strictly home-style - not a gourmet bone in my body There! Done!
(She places last jar in box, folds flaps up so that the audience can read the label: Elders and on second box: Sister missionaries.)
Why don't you ride along with me to deliver this.
(On phone)
Why don't I pick you up on my way to deliver these care packages?

Family Frolics, Relief Society Renditions and Sharing Time Skits -- Resource Manual

PIONEER CHILDREN
by Charlee Cardon Wilson

CHARACTERS
-- 4 male, 3 female

BOB, age 17-young adult
AMBER, age 4-7.
MARIE, age 17-young adult,
SCOTT, age 5-10.
DAN, age 14-16
KELLY, female, age 14-16
TIM, male, teen to young adult

NOTES
Be sure your cast fills in the "dead" places with ad libs (i.e. When a reaction of surprise is required from all cast members, they should ad lib a few of their own words rather than a Greek chorus-type "What?".) Block the skit with characters standing, sitting and moving around the stage as appropriate. Be sure those who are not speaking don't stand around doing nothing. They should look natural and participate through facial expressions and body movement.

[Stage is set as simply or as elaborately as resources permit. A full painted backdrop may be used, or bushes and grass may be painted on a few poster boards and propped up in various places. Potted plants and real "trees" (pruned branches) are very effective used in combination with or without full backdrop. An outdoor setting at a picnic or campfire program is ideal. Dead branches (firewood) and rocks are placed randomly. A log or two stones large enough to sit on are center stage. Enter BOB carrying AMBER piggy-back. MARIE follows with SCOTT. They are followed by DAN pulling a child's wagon which has been decorated to look like a covered wagon. KELLY is the last to enter. All are wearing pioneer clothes.]

BOB: *(sets Amber down slightly left of center stage and stretches)* Okay, troops, let's take a breather.
   (Marie and Kelly sink down wearily on the log center stage. Amber and Scott follow Dan as he makes an elaborate circle left of center stage with the wagon.)
DAN: circle the wagon!
KELLY: That wasn't funny the first hundred times you said it. Now it's beginning to be downright annoying!
AMBER: I'm hungry.

SCOTT: Me too. Can we have another sandwich?

BOB: Sounds good to me. Marie, why don't you rustle us up a snack while I go on ahead and scout around.

(He starts to walk off stage right, but stops as Marie speaks.)

MARIE: Hold it just a second, Tonto. I'd like to have a small pow-wow with you.

(To others)

You guys know the rules. Pioneers didn't stop for sandwiches every five minutes. Dan, you and Kelly take the little ones and go back to that big pine we just passed. There were lots of wild strawberries there.

BOB: Yeah, the currants were on too.

MARIE: Here, eat all you want, but bring back a few for us too.

(She removes bonnet and hands it to Kelly)

You can carry them in here.

KELLY: *(sighs, and rises reluctantly)* Okay, come on you guys. This ought to be exciting.

AMBER: Are we having fun yet?

BOB: *(As children begin to exit, Dan pulling wagon)* Hey, don't eat anything but strawberries and currants. Not all wild berries are edible, you know.

(Children exit stage right)

MARIE: *(arms folded, standing stiffly)* More inherited wisdom from "Heap Great-Grandfather", I suppose.

BOB: Yeah, well, I've been reading your smoke signals for the past half hour now, and it's easy to tell you're on the warpath about something. Now, are you gonna tell me, or do you want to act it out, and I'll guess.

MARIE: Come one now, Charades is too Mickey Mouse for a big-time game player like yourself. It doesn't have enough realism, enough machoism...

(She's groping for words)

... enough...Mosquitoes!

(She slaps her cheek in irritation, looks at her hand, then rubs it on her skirt.)

These things are eating me alive. I'm going to need a transfusion at this rate.

BOB: Yeah, well if griping were a Olympic event, you'd be a gold medalist. Here, didn't I tell you to rub some mint leaves on your skin.

(He looks around, finds some and picks it. Then, goes to her as if to rub it on.)

That'll keep 'em off.

MARIE: *(Backs off rapidly)* Oh no, no more of your old Indian remedies!

BOB: This happens to be a trick Euell Gibbons taught me. You have heard of Euell Gibbons...the great white naturalist.

MARIE: You mean the late Euell Gibbons. The great, white, deceased naturalist. That's some kind of great advertising wouldn't you say....Besides, the last "mint" you so kindly pointed out happened to be stinging nettle. Remember!

(She thrusts out her arm.)

It's still itches!

BOB: *(Sighs)* Okay, okay, I get the picture. You've got itchy skin, and you're anemic. I'm sorry, anything else?

MARIE: Yes! I've also got blisters on my feet, a third-degree sunburn on my nose, and cockle-burrs in my underwear! It's going to take the paramedics hours to cut me out of these ridiculous clothes. Everything is all stuck together underneath.
> *(She tugs savagely at her skirt which is pinned to her socks and bunched badly. Staples work well)*

BOB: Well, don't take it out on me. I didn't choose your foot-wear. Besides, if you'd worn your bonnet like a good pioneer...

MARIE: Right! Exactly like a good pioneer. Wasn't that the guys idea to be authentic? The guys, who got to wear normal clothing, while the good, authentic pioneer girls got to wear the really fun stuff! Ouch!
> *(She tugs at skirt, sits down abruptly, and begins to pick cockle-burrs out of her hem.)*

Oh Bob Braithwaite, if my petticoats weren't stuck to my shoelaces, I'd kick your shins right up between your shoulder blades!

BOB: *(Patiently)* Okay, okay,
> *(He kneels down and begins to help pull out burrs)*

got it all out of your system now? You know, you gripe more than the little kids.

MARIE: *(Matter of factly)* The little kids don't know we're lost, either.

BOB: *(Startled)* Lost?

MARIE: What, you were hoping nobody'd notice, right? Well, I'm no Cochise, but even I know that it was supposedly two and a half miles from the starting point to the ward picnic site. We've walked at least twice that far.

BOB: You're just out of condition. It only seems longer because you're not used to it.

MARIE: Okay, so explain this one, Geronimo...According to plan, the races and games were to start at 3:30, thus allowing for the "pioneer families" to make their trek and kick off the festivities. Of course, being a good authentic pioneer, I didn't wear my wrist watch, but even a dumb old paleface like myself can tell by looking at the position of the sun, that it's fast pushing toward evening.

BOB: Okay, so we got a little off the beaten path. We'll find it pretty soon. In fact, I'm almost sure I know where we are now.

MARIE: And if you're wrong?
> *(She affects macho Indian accent)*

Big Chief hunt buffalo, squaws dig roots, pick berries for winter?

BOB: For cryin' out loud, Marie, will you can the Indian jokes, please?

MARIE: Who's the one who regaled us with tales of his big chief ancestor all morning?

BOB: Okay, so I laid it on a little thick, I admit it, but I'm hollering "uncle" now.

You win! I give! Can we please call a truce and figure out what we're going to do?

MARIE: All right, peace brother.
> *(Bob gives her a threatening look, she looks back innocently)*

Uh, just how lost are we?

BOB: Lost doesn't come in degrees, Marie. It's like dead. You either are or you aren't.

MARIE: Now that's a cheering analogy. Let me rephrase the question. Just how long have we been lost?

BOB: Well, I'm not exactly sure....

MARIE: *(sighs)* Okay, let's try to determine the last time we weren't lost, then. May I see the map?

BOB: Well...er..that's kind of the problem.

MARIE: You lost the map.
> *(It's a statement.)*

BOB: Not exactly. Dan was carrying it.

MARIE: Dan lost the map?

BOB: No, it's just...well, remember when he fell in the creek?

MARIE: The map washed away.

BOB: Not all of it....just the writing part. It was all in felt tip.

MARIE: Terrific! So, we've been lost since Dan fell in the creek.
> *(Realization dawns)*

Bob! That was hours ago! We should have turned back and followed the highway down. Why didn't you tell me?

BOB: Well, I was going to, but then we met that fisherman, and he drew me a new map - said it was a clearly marked trail.....

MARIE: *(She's been trying to remember a fisherman)* Fisherman? Oh no, you don't mean that guy with all the empty beer cans?

BOB: Well, he seemed to know the country. He said it wasn't a hard trail to follow. Trouble is, I can't find any of the landmarks he wrote down.

MARIE: May I see the new map, please?

BOB: *(Shows it to her pointing out their route.)* See, there should have been a meadow of blue flowers just after we crossed the stream. Then the trail sort of zig-zags for a ways until it goes between two big trees.....

MARIE: Well, to begin with, those blue flowers were probably in bloom early last spring. This is the 24th of July. They'd be long gone by now. As for the zig-zagging trail and two trees, in his condition, he probably couldn't walk a straight line if his life depended on it, and I'll bet he sees two of everything. This map is useless.

BOB: You're right. I should have turned back. Maybe we'd better gather up the little kids and start back now.

MARIE: I don't think that's wise. It's too far. We'd never make it before dark, besides, we might get off the trail we came on.

BOB: Well, what's our alternative? We can't very well follow the stream down

to the lake. That's a good ten miles. Then we'd have to hike clear around to the lodge to a phone. Even if we got there, who would we call?
MARIE: We could stay right here until someone realizes we're lost and sends out search parties.
BOB: Oh man, you mean, let ourselves be rescued like a bunch of wimpy little city kids?
MARIE: I hate to point this out, but we are a bunch of wimpy little city kids. It's no disgrace. Even the authentic pioneers got lost occasionally.
BOB: Marie, it's going to be dark. It's already getting chilly. We don't have flashlights or matches or....
MARIE: Well, I cheated....I know it's not exactly authentic, but I brought my first aid kit. It has a penlight and matches and we've got jackets in the wagon. We could build a fire and wait.
BOB: Okay, maybe you're right. Look, you gather up the kids and get a fire going. I'll jog back the way we came and bring help.
MARIE: And leave me here with the lions and tigers and bears? No way!
BOB: What difference does it make whether I'm here or not. I don't have a gun.
MARIE: No, but you'd make a dandy first course, and maybe they'd be too full for dessert.
BOB: Thanks a lot.
(Voices are heard offstage.)
MARIE: Uh-oh, I hear the others. What are we going to do about them? I don't want a bunch of panicky kids to take of.
BOB: There's only one thing we can do...use old white man trick.
MARIE: What?
BOB: Speak with forked tongue.
MARIE: You mean lie.
BOB: Like a rug, lady, like a rug.
(Enter Dan, Kelly, Scott, and Amber. They do not have the wagon. Scott is carrying the bonnet.)
SCOTT: Okay, we ate up all the strawberries. Now can we have another sandwich?
MARIE: *(Takes bonnet)* Hey, I thought you guys were gonna bring some back. Where are they?
DAN: Do you know how long it would take to fill up that bonnet with wild strawberries.
SCOTT: Yeah man. They're so small you need a telescope to see them.
DAN: Microscope, dummy.
SCOTT: Whatever. Anyhow, they're real little.
BOB: What about the currants? I saw lots of them.
KELLY: Yeah, and every single one of 'em was occupied.
AMBER: What's occupied?
SCOTT: It means they had squirmy, slimy, little worms inside 'em.

(He lunges at Amber who squeals and hides behind Kelly.)
MARIE: Gross! Scott!
BOB: Hey, you guys wouldn't have made very good pioneers. They weren't so picky about what they ate.
AMBER: Yeah, but there wasn't no such a thing as worms in the olden days.
KELLY: Is that so? Where do you think those worms came from then, Smarty-pants?
AMBER: Pullootion. (Pollution)
I saw it on TV.
DAN: Worms! One more example of what mankind has unleashed on the ecological system.
BOB: Hey, gang, I've been saving up a little surprise for you.
(He and Marie exchange glances)
ALL: What?
AMBER: I hope it's Twinkies.
BOB: Nope, better than that...we're going to set up a real pioneer camp right here.
KELLY: What about the ward picnic? Are we going to miss it?
BOB: Actually, we're going to be a part of the games. We set up camp, and they have to guess where. The first ones who find us win.
DAN: Well, let's not stop here. Come on, let's find somewhere that they'll really have to look for.
MARIE: Oh no....we don't want it to be too tough on them.
BOB: Okay, now it's getting dark, so we need to be ready. You girls go gather up firewood. The guys and I will get some rocks and clear a place for our campfire.
(Kids start gathering up rocks and wood around stage.)
Then we can tell stories and sing songs like the pioneers did.
SCOTT: Are you gonna tell us more stories about your Great Grandpa? That Indian guy?
DAN: *(Groans)* Gee, I can hardly wait.
AMBER: What kind of Indian was he, Bobby?
MARIE: *(Sweetly)* Wasn't he one of the lost ten tribes?
BOB: *(Warning)* Marie.
AMBER: I heard of them. They're famous.
KELLY: What time were they supposed to start this hide and seek game? I'm tired of being a pioneer.
MARIE: Tell me about it. I never realized how much I love my jeans. Even my grubby ones are nicer than these.
KELLY: How did girls stand wearing long, hot dresses day after day?
AMBER: I bet they were awful soccer players.
SCOTT: *(Places the last rock in a circle center stage.)* How's that, Bob?
BOB: Yeah, looking good there. Okay, Dan, you better get the matches.
KELLY: Hey, get my jacket too. It's getting cold out here.

DAN: Where is all this stuff?
BOB: The first aid kit is in the wagon...right, Marie?
MARIE: *(Looking around)* Yeah, right under my jacket..Hey, where is the wagon?
DAN: Oh no. Scott, you were supposed to pull the wagon back. Didn't you bring it?
SCOTT: I wasn't supposed to. I had to carry the bonnet. Kelly was supposed to.
KELLY: Not me. You wear the pants, you pull the wagon.
BOB: Hey, hey, no big deal. Dan and I will just run back and get it.
MARIE: Oh no you don't. You're the first course, remember. Scott's a big boy, he can help.
BOB: Well, hurry, you two. It's getting dark. You won't be able to find your way back.
MARIE: There's a penlight in the first aid kit. Use it.
SCOTT: I get to hold the flashlight.
 (He and Dan argue as they exit'stage right.)
KELLY: I sure hope somebody finds us fast. I don't want to miss the dance. How long do we have to stick around here, anyway? Isn't there some kind of time limit, Bob?
BOB: Well, we have to offer them a fair chance, don't we?
MARIE: Besides, how can you even think about dancing after all the abuse our feet have taken today?
AMBER: She just wants to dance with Tim. They don't hardly even move. They just stand there and make moony-eyes at each other.
KELLY: Amber, watch it! Mom told you to quit'saying that in front of everybody.
MARIE: It's not like it was some big secret, Kelly. Anybody with eyes can see you two are a item.
KELLY: Yeah, well the why didn't they put Tim in our wagon train instead of Carrie Fowlers' bunch?
BOB: Uh-oh, jealousy rears her ugly head.
KELLY: I'm not jealous. I just feel sorry for poor Tim with Carrie drooling over him all day.
BOB: The idea behind this whole exercise was to help us appreciate our pioneer ancestors. It was not a match-making venture.
KELLY: Still, it wouldn't have hurt anything if Tim had come with our group.
AMBER: I'm hungry. I don't think I want to play pioneers any more. Can't we go to the picnic now?
BOB: Hey, this is gonna be fun. We'll have a fire and eat sandwiches and sing songs....
AMBER: Okay, you guys keep playing. I'll go back to the picnic and I promise I won't tell anybody where you are.
 (She starts to leave.)
BOB: Hey, the pioneers couldn't quit when they were tired.

(He picks her up carries her to log and sits down with her on his lap.)
They still had to be pioneers, right? Come on, you're a good pioneer, right?
AMBER: But...
MARIE: Come on, let's sing something.
KELLY: *(Sings)* Pioneer children sang as they walked and walked and....
MARIE: Not that one, please....um, how about
(sings) **Come, come ye saints**
(All join in singing. Enter Scott and Tim. If desired, Dan may return eliminating the extra character. See alternate dialogue at the end of the skit.)
TIM: Hey, it's a good thing you guys started singing. We'd have walked right past you.
KELLY: Tim! What are you doing here?
TIM: I could ask you that question. Dan said something about some kind of hide and seek game....
SCOTT: Hey, nobody's lookin' for us.
TIM: Sorry, Bob, somebody dropped the ball. We didn't know we were supposed to be looking for you. In fact, if Carrie and I hadn't run into Dan, you guys could have sat out here all night.
KELLY: You and Carrie? What were you and Carrie doing?
TIM: Aw, that crazy Carrie, she's been on my back for the last two hours. She was sure you guys were hurt or lost or something. You know how melodramatic she can get....
SCOTT: Boy, you should have seen her...
(Mimics damsel in distress in a falsetto voice.)
Oh Tim, whatever would I do without you. You're so strong and handsome....
KELLY: *(Enraged)* What?
SCOTT: There he was, trying to carry her through the brush....
KELLY: *(Looking from Scott to Tim in disbelief.)* Carry? You carried Carrie?
SCOTT: Hey, that's a good one. Carry Carrie.
(Laughs)
TIM: Cool it, Scott.
SCOTT: Yeah, well if you hadn't run into us and the wagon, you'd have had to carry her all the way back to camp.
KELLY: You carried Carrie?
AMBER: You already said that.
TIM: She hurt her ankle. What was I supposed to do?
KELLY: You were supposed to hold up your little hand like this...
(Demonstrates movements she describes - a farewell wave.)
...wiggle your little fingers like this, and say "Bye bye, Fathead. I'll see you back at camp!" That's what you were supposed to do.
TIM: Come on, what if her ankle's broken?
KELLY: Better yet, you could have shot her.
BOB: My, what a touching display of Christian charity....May I suggest you continue this discussion later? Tim, you know the way back?

TIM: Well, sure, it's just back there a ways. You guys weren't hidden too well. Your fire could have been seen from the road real easy.

MARIE: Then why couldn't we hear anyone?

TIM: Oh, you'll hear them pretty soon. The slide show has been going on for about 45 minutes. Before that, Brother Davis talked about the hand cart companies. They should be starting the singing any minute. You'd have heard them for sure then. Are you coming back now? It's kinda late to start folks looking for anything. It's too dark to see very well.

BOB: Gee, guess we have no choice....I mean if they're not going to do the search part....

MARIE: I feel silly sitting out here waiting. I'll bet people began to wonder if we were lost or something.

TIM: Nah! Only that crazy Carrie. After all, everybody knows Bob's ancestors were Indians. He couldn't get lost if he tried.

(All exit as curtain falls.)

(THE END)

OR
ALTERNATE DIALOGUE FOR DAN

(Dan and Scott enter without the wagon.)

DAN: Hey, it's a good thing you guys started singing, we'd have walked right past you.

BOB: Where's the wagon?

AMBER: Where's my coat. I'm cold.

SCOTT: Hey, nobody's looking for us.

BOB: Where's the wagon?

DAN: Hold your horses everybody.

(All quiet)

Tim has the wagon.

KELLY: Tim? You saw Tim? Where is he?

(She looks around.)

DAN: That's what he asked us...where were we? Hey Bob, somebody dropped the ball. Nobody knew they were supposed to look for us. If we hadn't run into Tim and Carrie, we could have been sitting here all night.

KELLY: Tim and Carrie? What was Tim doing with Carrie?

DAN: Aw, that crazy Carrie. She's been on his back for the past two hours. She was sure we were all hurt or lost or something. You know how melodramatic she gets...

SCOTT: Boy, you should have seen her...

(Mimics damsel in distress in a falsetto voice.)

Oh Tim, whatever would I do without you. You're so strong and handsome....

KELLY: What!

SCOTT: There he was, trying to carry her through the brush...

KELLY: (looking from Scott to Dan in disbelief) Carry? He carried Carrie? Hey, that's a good one. Carry Carrie.
    (Laughs)
DAN: Cool it, Scott.
SCOTT: Yeah, well, if he hadn't run into us and the wagon, he'd have had to carry her all the way back to camp.
KELLY: He carried Carrie!
AMBER: You already said that.
DAN: She hurt her ankle. What was he supposed to do.
KELLY: He was supposed to hold up his little hand like this...
    (Demonstrates movements she describes - a farewell wave)
...wiggle his little fingers like this, and say "Bye bye Fathead. I'll see you back at camp!" That's what he was supposed to do.
DAN: Come on, what if her ankle's broken.
KELLY: Better yet, he could have shot her.
BOB: My, what a touching display of Christian charity...do you suppose you could continue this later. Uh, Dan do you know the way back to camp?
DAN: Well sure, it's just back there a ways. I told you we weren't hidden very well. Our fire could have been seen from the road real easy.
MARIE: Then, why couldn't we hear anyone?
DAN: Oh, we'll hear them pretty soon. Tim says the slide show has been going on for about 45 minutes. Before that, Brother Davis talked about the hand cart companies. They're supposed to start singing any time. We'd have heard them for sure then. Hey, Bob, what are we going to do? It's kinda late to start folks looking. It's getting too dark to see very well.
BOB: Gee, guess we have no choice...I mean if they're not going to do the search part....
MARIE: I feel silly sitting out here waiting. I'll bet people began to wonder if we were lost or something.
DAN: Nah! Only that crazy Carrie. After all, everybody knows Bob's ancestors were Indians. He couldn't get lost if he tried.
    (All exit as curtain falls.)

*(**THE END**)*

THE RELUCTANT SHEPHERD
by
James G. Lambert

CHARACTERS
RUBEN--the father
NAOMI--the mother
ISAAC--the oldest son
HEZBA--the oldest daughter
ESTER--the youngest daughter
SAUL--the youngest son
ANGELS
OTHER **SHEPHERDS**
MARY
JOSEPH

SCENE ONE *On a hillside near Bethlehem. Naomi sits by a fire as Ruben enters in a huff.*

RUBEN: Naomi! where is that boy?
NAOMI: Saul? I do not know, Ruben. You should have sent Isaac.
RUBEN: It's time Saul took on some responsibility. I warrant he's off somewhere dreaming.
NAOMI: He may be lying somewhere bleeding to death. I've heard there are thieves about trying to intercept Caesar's taxes.
RUBEN: They'd hardly try to steal the few crumbs Saul would be carrying.
NAOMI: I You don't know that for sure.
ISAAC: Saul isn't back yet?
RUBEN: No, and who gave you permission to leave the sheep?
ISAAC: I'm tired and I'm hungry. Besides, Hezba and Esther are still there.
RUBEN: You would leave all the work to your sisters?
ISAAC: They can watch the sheep as well as I can.
NAOMI: But what if there is trouble?
ISAAC: Then they will scream and we will come running.
RUBEN: Go back out until you're called in.
ISAAC: If you're worried--you go!
NAOMI: Isaac! Apologize!
(Calms Ruben at the same time)
ISAAC: I'm sorry, Father.
NAOMI: Why! Isaac?
ISAAC: I'm sick of doing Saul's work as well as my own. He never does his

share!
NAOMI: But he's just a boy, you are a young man!
  (Silence a moment)
ISAAC: I'm tired and hungry. Is there any food yet?
RUBEN: No, not until Saul gets back. We are all hungry.
ISAAC: Can't I sleep 'til he arrives?
  (Lies down)
RUBEN: Two sons I have. One is a dreamer, the other is lazy.
  (Exits)
NAOMI: Won't you try harder to obey your father? You are his first born! Would you lose your birthright?
ISAAC: I have nothing to fear. Saul has no hope of ever becoming a good shepherd.
NAOMI: He may yet grow up and fool us all.
ISAAC: Not in two lifetimes.
ESTER: *(Entering)* Still no sign of Saul?
NAOMI: No and I am quite worried.
ESTER: So you want me to go look for him?
NAOMI: No. Too many things could happen to a pretty little girl like you.
ESTER: Why don't you go Isaac?
ISAAC: Am I my brother's keeper? Let him fend for himself.
ESTER: How can you be so cruel?
ISAAC: Quit blubbering over Saul and get back out to the flock where you belong--unless you want to feel my hand.
NAOMI: Isaac!
ESTER: *(Exiting)* Aren't we brave tonight.
ISAAC: *(Starts to rise in anger but sees Ester has gone)* Saul just might amount to something one day if that one would quit trying to baby him.
NAOMI: Ester means well.
ISAAC: So do the Romans. They're a blight on our country
NAOMI: Careful! Isaac, you never know who might be listening. Such talk is dangerous.
ISAAC: Who would be out there now?
SAUL: *(Offstage)* I am.
  (Isaac and Naomi both act startled at first then Saul enters. Isaac's concern turns to anger and he grabs Saul)
ISAAC: Where have you been?
SAUL: Home.
ISAAC: *(Shaking Saul)* Don't get smart. You've had time to get home and back three times. And where is our food?
SAUL: I didn't bring any.
  (ISAAC hits Saul and knocks him to the ground)
ISAAC: What? You ate it all yourself, didn't you?

(No answer)
Well?
SAUL: No.
RUBEN: *(Entering with Hezba)* What's the meaning of this?
ISAAC: Saul came back without our food.
RUBEN: What? Why?
(Ester reenters)
ISAAC: Who knows? He isn't explaining anything!
RUBEN: Be quiet and give him a chance to speak for himself! What happened, Saul?
SAUL: I tried to do what you asked me, I just couldn't.
RUBEN: Why not?
SAUL: There wasn't enough.
ISAAC: See, he ate it all himself!
SAUL: No, I didn't. I didn't eat a bite.
NAOMI: Were you robbed?
SAUL: No nothing like that.
HEZBA: Can't you see he's stalling? Make him tell!
RUBEN: Your sister is right. Where is our food?
SAUL: It's gone.
HEZBA: Gone where?
SAUL: It's been eaten?
HEZBA: By who--you?
ESTER: Hezba, he's your brother. He already told you he didn't eat the food. Stop attacking him!
HEZBA: Not until he tells us everything.
RUBEN: All of you be quiet! The only voice I want to hear is Saul's' and he had better be brief! Saul?
SAUL: As I said, there really wasn't enough for us for a meal. I knew, if we had to, we could always butcher a lamb! so--I gave it to some people in need.
RUBEN: You gave our food away?
SAUL: Yes, you should have seen them, father.
RUBEN: By what right do you give away our food?
SAUL: When you sent me to get it you made me responsible for it until I came back. I used that responsibility as I thought best. They needed food so much worse than we did.
RUBEN: Who did?
SAUL: A carpenter and his wife, come all the way from Nazareth to Bethlehem to pay their taxes.
RUBEN: A carpenter, with taxes to pay, should have been able to pay for a meal.
SAUL: He could have payed if he could have found space at one of the inns. They were all full as are all the houses with those who have come to pay their taxes.

ISAAC: I still don't see why we should have to give up our food for them.
SAUL: His wife is with child and suffered much from their travel here.
HEZBA: Did you at least charge him for their meals?
SAUL: No, I couldn't
ISAAC: Where are these people now?
SAUL: Sleeping, in our manger.
RUBEN: In our manger? Why there?
SAUL: Because there was no place other than our house and I dared not put them in there.
HEZBA: Why not? You've given them everything else!
SAUL: Because I was sure you wouldn't let then stay there alone.
RUBEN: You knew what you were doing was wrong.
SAUL: No, I knew it was right to help these people, only you wouldn't think so.
RUBEN: I see. You are right and I am wrong now?
SAUL: Go and meet them before you make a final judgement. See if you would not have done the same.
RUBEN: That is enough, Saul. Don't add to your punishment by trying to put me in the wrong.
ESTER: Father, please don't punish him. He was doing what he thought was right.
RUBEN: Ester, he has earned what he will receive. Stay out of it.
(To Saul)
You know the position well son, bend over!
(Saul bends over to receive punishment. He is blocked from the audience by Naomi, Isaac, Hezba and Ruben, who using his staff, applies two blows to Saul's backside. Ester cannot watch and turns to see a light in the sky.)
ESTER: Father, look! What is that light in the sky?
RUBEN: *(Turning)* Ester, I told you

MUSICAL NUMBER Hark the Herald Angels Sing! (1st x hum 2nd x sing)

(Ruben stares in awe, others look on in stages of fear and interest as a Heavenly Choir is heard first humming and then singing)
NAOMI: *(In awe)* Can it be true? The Savior is born?
ESTER: It must be true. Can you deny the signs? Let us go and find him!
HEZBA: It's the only way we could know for sure.
RUBEN: Let us go into Bethlehem.
ISAAC: You go. I'll stay with the sheep.
NAOMI: Isaac, you should not miss this.
SAUL: I'll stay with the sheep if someone must.
ISAAC: I have no desire to go off on some wild journey!
ESTER: After what we've seen and heard, how can you say that?
ISAAC: I've seen mirages before.
RUBEN: At night--with singing voices?

ISAAC: Maybe it wasn't a mirage but I'm sure it was something just as easily explained.
NAOMI: Don't say that, Isaac!
ISAAC: Go! All of you, go! Leave me alone!
RUBEN: Let us go. No reason we should miss it because the boy is unwilling to admit the miracle we have seen. Come!
(All but Isaac exit. Isaac shows disgust, then lies down as lights fade out.)

SCENE TWO--THE MANGER

MUSICAL NUMBER Away in a Manger

(As song is sung we see the nativity scene. Mary, Joseph and the Christ Child in a bed of straw. Shepherds enter bearing gifts of food and homespun. Finally Ruben, Naomi, Hezba, Ester and Saul enter. All but Saul go to kneel by the Christ Child. Saul is met by Joseph who greets him warmly and take him to see the Child. As they come to stand near Ruben, Ruben turns to look at Saul. Saul looks lovingly at his father, who, still on his knees gathers his son to him. The preceding action should be carefully timed to the music)

MUSICAL NUMBER Joy to the World

(THE END)

Family Frolics, Relief Society Renditions and Sharing Time Skits -- Resource Manual

THE VISITING TEACHING LEADER
by
Charlee Cardon Wilson

CHARACTERS
Narrator
4 Visiting Teachers -- Tillie, Polly, Connie, Mathilda
Relief Society President (actual)
Child

This presentation, appropriate for visiting Teaching Luncheons, Relief Society dinners, and Ward and Stake meetings, is read by a narrator. A large frame is on the stage with a spotlight shining on it. As each teacher is being described, she poses in the frame as directed. This is all done in fun, and the introduction of this skit may want to emphasize that fact. I have been all of these visiting teachers at one time or another. The narrator stands on the floor with a hand mike. Curtain opens with Visiting Teaching Leader #1 already posed in frame. She starts out fresh and smiling. An Avon Lady advertisement, but she becomes a bit frayed around the edges as the scene progresses.

NARRATOR: The calling of a visiting teaching leader is a uniquely challenging one. There is much more to the position than preparing a lesson once a month and writing reports. For instance, assigning the right sisters to a route can be a problem. Mistakes come back to haunt her. Even deciding which sisters should be visiting teaching partners can be a problem. I remember one visiting teaching leader, who, going on the assumption that "opposites attract" assigned Nervous Nellie and Fearless Faye to a route together. Faye demonstrated how she could drive down (your areas busiest street) at rush hour and not have to stop for a single light. Nellie's stutter became so pronounced that she couldn't give the message. Following this fiasco, the visiting teaching leader changed her philosophy and looked for partners with common interest. She discovered the flaw in that line of thinking the night that she received two irate phone calls from the supperless husbands of Chatty Kathy and Gabbie Gertie. They had left on their rounds at 9:30 that morning and still were unaccounted for at seven PM Nevertheless, it's through experiences such as these that she learns and grows.
    (Visiting Teaching Leader in frame is no longer smiling as brightly, but on the "learns and grows" line, she squares her shoulders and puts determined look on her face.)
Perhaps the greatest learning experience our VTL can have is having to

cope with the dread Visiting Teacher's Virus. The symptoms of this disease range from a cold, to morning sickness, to six children with chicken pox, and in rare cases have included twin daughters having twin wedding receptions. Regardless of the severity of the symptoms, the results are the same. The afflicted teacher discovers sometime between the 28th and the last day of the month, that due to circumstances beyond her control, she cannot make her rounds. In mild cases, the disease affects only five per cent of the teachers in a single ward. More often than not, it occurs in epidemic proportions, knocking out ninety to one hundred percent of the staff. It is in the latter case that the VTL finds herself with a monumental task. Armed with a ward list, a map, and an eighteen-hour girdle, she sets out to deliver the monthly message to 182 homes.

>*(Visiting Teaching Leader who had run her hands through her hair mussing it'slightly, juggles ward list, opens map, and tugs sharply at her 'girdle' pulling it up and her skirt down. She's beginning to sag a little.)*

During the course of her day, she visits a home with a large and ferocious dog. Although she's always felt inadequate when participating in track and field events, she discovers a speed and agility previously hidden for lack of proper incentive.

>*(VTL turns map so that audience an see large bite taken out of it. She adjusts her purse she's been carrying to reveal a large muddy spot on her dress. She runs hands through hair to muss it further. If a cuff of a sleeve can be quickly detached and left hanging, it adds to the effect.)*

She also discovers an eloquence she'd never known when she must present the monthly message 182 times with freshness and vitality. The experience teachers her map reading.

>*(VTL assumes pose with all her stuff juggled, squinting at map and scratching her head. If she can manage to get hose to sag creating elephant legs, do it.)*

She becomes better acquainted with, while not more appreciative of city planning. She learns which filling station attendants will cheerfully give directions even if one doesn't need gas. She discovers that despite what her husband has told her, when the gas gauge reads empty, there is not a quarter of a tank left. In short, she learns to endure to the end, bitter though it may be.

>*(VTL, thoroughly beaten, drags herself off the stage, trailing paraphernalia behind her.)*

THE VISITING TEACHERS
TWO MINUTE TILLIE

>*(Tillie enters wearing jogging suit, carrying a stop watch and any other jogging accoutrements that can be acquired She begins warm-up exercises.)*

Tillie comes from a long line of pony express riders and efficiency experts. She was born with time in one hand and a schedule box in the other.

Operating on the theory that there is no visiting teaching route that cannot benefit from a rigid schedule, every month becomes a new challenge for her. Indeed, she looks on her route as an Olympic event, trying each month to better the previous month's time. Is.it possible to cut fifteen seconds off her traveling time by driving through the shopping center parking lot rather than taking a chance with the light and the corner?

(Tillie is now busy making calculations, checking her watch and writing in a schedule book.)

Does a knock bring a faster response than ringing the doorbell? She makes a careful analysis of her route watching for any little change that might win her an extra minute or two.

(Tillie begins crossing out lines in her manual with great slashes.)

Tillie gives the Stake's only Reader's Digest Condensed version of the visiting teaching message. Her record time for a visit is one minute forty-two seconds. She allows thirty seconds for "How are you?"; sixty seconds for her message and another thirty seconds for "See you next month."

(Tillie continues warm-up exercises, taking pulse, stretching, etc.)

While it's true that Tillie s system is incredibly efficient, it does have it's drawbacks. For instance, in checking her watch one month, she neglected to notice that Sister Clutterbumph was wearing a neck brace and body cast. It wasn't until Brother Clutterbumph called the Relief Society President to inquire whether he could wash sweat socks with dandruff shampoo that anyone realized the good sister needed a hand with the housework. Then, there was the new convert on Tillie's route who was totally baffled by Tillie's visits. As a matter of fact, the new Sister thought for several months that Tillie was a friendly, fast talking sale representative.

(Tillie assumes race starting position.)

Rather than feeling spiritually enriched by her visits, she merely felt relieved that she managed to avoid buying anything from her.

(Starting gun is fired, and Tillie sprints off.)

POLLY PROCRASTINATION

(Narrator announces Polly, waits a moment while nothing happens, and announces her again. The Relief Society President walks out has a brief conference with the Narrator, checks her watch, and shrugs her shoulders, and walks off. Narrator is a little flustered.)

Uh...It doesn't appear that she's here, yet. I guess we'll just go ahead...

(Looks to President who nods and shrugs.)

Polly was born four weeks late. Even then, her tired Mother thought it was just another false alarm, so she put off going to the hospital until it was too late. Since then, Polly has been arriving on every scene a day late and and a dollar short. She faithfully attends her visiting teaching meetings every month, always arriving in time for the closing prayer. Polly's motto is: Never put off until tomorrow what you can put off until the thirtieth of the month.

Consequently, she has a perfect record for never getting her February visits made. She's meant to get a calendar for several years, but she always waits until July when they're half-price. If it weren't for Sister Polly, the calling of Visiting Teaching Leader could be dull indeed. As it is, she brings an element of suspense into the otherwise hum-drum routine. We're sorry she couldn't be with us today. She seems to have been delayed. Oh, while we're on the subject, the Relief Society Presidency has asked me to make the following announcement:

(Narrator unfolds note and reads.)

It has come to our attention that a few of the sisters have been making wagers on whether Sister Polly will make her rounds in time each month. Even though the stakes involved are only babysitting, and not negotiable currency, the sisters should know that it is still considered gambling and is therefore a definite no-no. Thank you!

CASUAL CONSTANCE

(Connie enters wearing old clothes, preferably army issue with lots of pockets. She has curlers in her hair and is wearing an old scarf or diaper over them.)

Unpretentious is the word for Connie. She's not the kind to put on airs. Her Sunday Best is only seen on Sunday. Her second best is reserved for all other church meetings, and as for her everyday attire....well, someone has to wear the odd socks and hubby's old-but-not-ready--for-the-rag-bag shirts. She has no use for ladies pants. Why, there's no wear in them at all, and worse, no pockets! How s a girl supposed to function without pockets? Connie made a most marvelous discovery in her quest for comfortable, but serviceable clothing. The army surplus store! Now there is somebody who really knows what the modern mother needs. Plenty of pockets

(Connie models)

reinforced seat and knees for gardening and scrubbing floors, and the shirts - well, if the day ever comes when hubby's cast-off supply is exhausted, she knows just where to go. It's true, the color selection is practically nil, but Connie's never been one for frills.

(Connie begins scrubbing floor on hands and knees)

When Connie's visiting teachers come, she welcomes them and invites them to share in her day. They've delivered the monthly message while lending a hand with the dishes, washing windows, folding clothes, weeding, and a multitude of other chores. As often as they've visited in Connie's home they've never found her sitting in the living room relaxing.

(Connie prepares herself to go out, she stuffs rags into her pockets, a whisk broom in her back pocket, and picks up a shovel.)

When Connie goes out on her own rounds, she goes prepared to work as her own visiting teachers do. The only addition she makes to her everyday ensemble is the few jumbo rollers in her hair topped by a bandanna. Usually, an old gauze diaper suffices. In the interest of water conservation, she dispenses with a shower and brushing her teeth, especially since she must do both later in the day. Unfortunately, Connie is still waiting for the chance to scrub a floor or wash a dish. The sisters on her route have an exasperating practice of ushering her into the parlor where they expect her to deliver the message and chat in totally unproductive manner. Still, she's hoping that someday she'll arrive to hear someone say, "Can you talk to me out back? I was just about to shovel out the barn.

(Connie grins and exits.)

MATERIAL MATHILDA

(Matilda poses with a baby [use a doll if you wish], and two small children clinging to her skirts. She is pregnant. She's serene.)

Matilda is first, last, and always a mother. She's on the job twenty-four hours a day. With seven preschool age children, she must be. She believes that children learn by doing. So comfortable in the knowledge that her offspring are storing up valuable experience for the future, she packs up the lot and sets out on her visiting teaching route. After four minutes in the air-conditioned family wagon, the little ones arrive at the first home in a state of advanced dehydration. While Matilda imparts her monthly message, they impart water all over the floor getting themselves ready for the next long, dry ride. Despite the puddles Matilda leaves behind, the sister is grateful for her genuine interest. She is also grateful that she is not the second stop on Matilda's route where Nature will demand that the cargo taken on be disposed of in the guest bath amid much flushing, washing with decorator soaps, and drying with assorted guest towels.

(Matilda bends sweetly and passes out candy to each child who proceeds to smear it all over faces and clothing.)

Realizing that the children are becoming restless, Mathilda supplies them all with a small treat before making the last two stops on her route. She's confident that the favorite chocolate candies (the kind that melt in your mouth, your hands, your hair, etc.) will keep the children quiet and happy for the duration. She then sets off to visit sisters Myrtle Meticulous and Irma Immaculate, neither of whom have small children. Matilda realizes they miss having little ones, because each time she leaves, the sisters have tears in their eyes. She resolves to spend extra time with each. Maternal Matilda is a model visiting teacher. She always leaves a sweet spirit in the homes she visits. Actually, once she left two sweet spirits and didn't miss them for almost forty-five minutes.

(Child whispers in Matilda's ear and points off stage. She smiles apologetically, takes children by the hand and exits.)

We are proud to enter the four visiting teachers presented today in our Visiting Teacher's Hall of Fame. There is much we can learn from their examples. We would do well to incorporate some of their better qualities into our own Visiting Teaching.

> *(Enter Tillie)*

Tillie, for instance, always calls the sisters on her route before she leaves. She takes the most direct route, makes no unnecessary stops, and never overstays her welcome.
Polly...

> *(Polly skids in panting and apologizing. Narrator holds up hand to silence her.)*

...Ahem, Polly, late though she may be,

> *(Polly smiles sheepishly)*

never misses her visiting teaching meetings.

> *(Enter Connie)*

Connie has a sincere desire to be of service to the sisters on her route, and

> *(Enter Matilda)*

Matilda, despite her large family, is never too busy to make her rounds or to show a genuine interest in the sisters she visits. May we suggest that each of us examine our own visiting teaching methods and see if we might not benefit from our four Hall of Famer's examples.

(THE END)

Family Frolics, Relief Society Renditions and Sharing Time Skits -- Resource Manual

A VOICE FROM THE DUST
by Charlee Cardon Wilson

CHARACTERS
Narrator
Moroni -- singing
Joseph -- singing
Choir (optional)

(This presentation is appropriate for missionary theme gatherings. Moroni is standing stage left, dressed in Book of Mormon attire. He is bruised and battle weary. He carries gold plates which he puts into a stone box at the end of his sketch. Joseph Smith, dressed in white, open collared shirt and dark; trousers stands stage right. If spotlights are available, the spot first comes up on Moroni during his part, then to Joseph. If no spots are used, the person not performing, stands quietly with his head down. A large screen is at the center back of the stage. If a very elaborate production is desired, substitute living paintings for slides or use in combination with slides, having costumed characters posed in frames around the hall. Spotlights come up on each frame as narration calls for it.)

MORONI: Now I, Moroni, have not as yet perished; and I make not myself known to the Lamanites lest they should destroy me. For behold, their wars are exceedingly fierce among themselves; and because of their hatred, they put to death every Nephite that will not deny the Christ. And I, Moroni, will not deny the Christ; wherefore, I wander whithersoever I can for the safety of mine own life. Wherefore, I write a few more things, that perhaps they may be of worth unto my brethren, the Lamanites, in some future day, according to the will of the Lord. And I seal up these records, after I have spoken a few words by way of exhortation unto you. "And when ye shall receive these things, I would exhort you that ye would ask God, the Eternal Father, in the name of Christ, if these things are not true; and if ye shall ask with a sincere heart, with real intent, having faith in Christ, he will manifest the truth of it unto you, by the power of the Holy Ghost. And by the power of the Holy Ghost, ye shall know the truth of all things..." And now, I bid unto all, farewell. I soon go to rest in the paradise of God, until my spirit and body shall again reunite, and I am brought forth to meet you before the pleasing bar of the great Jehovah, the Eternal Judge of both quick and dead, Amen.
  (He places plates in stone box, puts lid on box and bows his head for a moment, then, rises and speaks with great conviction.)
This work must go forth!

Family Frolics, Relief Society Renditions and Sharing Time Skits -- Resource Manual

MY BROTHER

My brother,
My heart cries out to thee across the sands of time.
My voice whispers to thee from the dust.
My brother,
Turn not thy face away, accept the call divine.
The salvation of this people is thy trust!
I'm weary.
My mission here is through and yours has not begun,
Yet my love, dear brother spans the years.
And verily,
The task is hard e'en though you are the chosen one.
The way is paved in sorrow, stained with tears.
Joseph,
Let not thy heart be troubled, shrink not from His sight.
Our loving Elder Brother plots the way.
And when the darkness threatens, He shall be thy light
To guide thee safely through the night to day.
How well I know
The loneliness and pain that fill thy soul with care.
My role is nearly finished, I seek rest.
Yet long ago,
Another claimed the sorrows we could never bear.
No greater love was ever manifest.

> *(Moroni bows head, slides or overhead projector flashes appropriate pictures from Book of Mormon or library while scriptures are read by narrator. Music may continue under narration with the theme changing to "Oh How Lovely Was the Morning" when Joseph in the grove is shown. The numbers in parentheses indicate the number of slides. See note at end of script)*

NARRATOR: And it came to pass that I beheld, and saw the people of the seed of my brethren (1) that they had overcome my seed; and they went forth in multitudes upon the face of the land. And I saw them gathered together in multitudes and I saw wars (2) and rumors of wars among them; and in wars and rumors of wars I saw many generations pass away. And the angel said unto me: 'Behold these (3) shall dwindle in unbelief.' And it came to pass that the angel spake unto me, saying: 'Look! And I looked and beheld (4) many nations and kingdoms. And he said unto me: These are the nations and kingdoms of the Gentiles. And it came to pass that I looked and beheld many waters; (5) and they divided the Gentiles from the seed of my brethren. And I beheld (6) a man among the Gentiles who was separated from the seed of my brethren my many waters; and I beheld the Spirit of

God, that it came down and wrought upon the man; and he went forth upon the many waters, even unto the seed of my brethren who were in the promised land. And it came to pass that I beheld many multitudes (7) of the Gentiles upon the land of promise and I beheld the wrath of God, that it was upon the seed of my brethren (8) and they were smitten. And the Gentiles did prosper and obtain the land for their inheritance. And I beheld a book, (9) and it was carried forth among them. And the angel said, 'The book that thou beholdest is a record of the Jews, which contains the covenants of the Lord, which he hath made unto the house of Israel; and it also containeth many of the prophecies of the holy prophets and it is a record like unto the engravings which are upon the plates of brass...wherefore, they are of great worth unto the Gentiles...The Gentiles do stumble exceedingly, because of the most plain and precious parts of the gospel of the Lamb which have been kept back. For behold, saith the Lamb: 'I will be merciful unto the Gentiles. I will bring forth unto them, in mine own power, (10) much of my gospel which shall be plain and precious...I will manifest myself unto thy seed, that they shall write many things which I shall minister unto them which shall be plain and precious, and after thy seed shall be destroyed, and dwindle in unbelief, and also the seed of thy brethren, behold, these things shall be hid up, to come forth unto the Gentiles, by the gift and Power of the Lamb. And in them shall be written my gospel, saith the Lamb, and my rock and my salvation.' And the angel spake unto me saying: 'These last records, (11) which thou hast seen among the Gentiles, shall establish the truth of the first, which are of the twelve apostles of the Lamb, and shall make known the plain and precious things which have been taken away from them; and shall make known to all kindreds tongues, and people, that the Lamb of God (12) the Son of the Eternal Father, and the Savior of the world; and that all men must come unto him, or they cannot be saved.

JOSEPH: (Bends over stone box, lifts out plates) And when ye shall receive these things, I would exhort you that ye would ask God, the Eternal Father in the name of Christ, if these things are not true; and if ye shall ask with a sincere heart, with real intent, having faith in Christ, he will manifest the truth of it unto you, by the power of the Holy Ghost. And by the power of the Holy Ghost, ye shall know the truth of all things.

(He looks up and says)
This work shall go forth!

MY BROTHER

My brother,
I hear the call with joy and clasp it to my breast
Though mortal weakness causes me to shake.
My brother,
A truth-starved world cries out to me, I cannot rest

The way is hard, but it's the path I take.
My brother
You did the task at hand, you did not turn away,
Though close around you enemies did press.
And others
Their voices raised with yours to reach this latter-day
Their spirits whisper I cannot do less.
Moroni,
My heart shall not be troubled, I'll not shrink from sight.
Our loving Elder Brother plots the way.
And when the darkness threatens, He shall be my light.
To guide me safely through the night to day.
The path is laid,
I'll go and do the things my Father asks of me.
I'll cry the good news: come, rejoice, repent!
I'm not afraid.
For should my voice be silenced by the enemy,
The blood they spill shall seal my testament.

 (spoken)
I will go and do the things which the Lord hath commanded, for I know that the Lord giveth no commandments unto the children of men, save he shall prepare a way for them that they may accomplish the thing which he commandeth them.

 (Joseph, Moroni, and optional chorus dressed in missionary clothes or a variety Book of Mormon, New and Old Testament clothes and modern wear join to sing, lifting their arms to the audience, inviting them to accept the call)

ALL:
MY BROTHERS
Our hearts cry out to thee across the sands of time,
Our voices whisper to thee from the dust.
My brothers,
Turn not thyselves away, accept the call divine.
The salvation of this people is thy trust.

 (Audience is invited to sing "The Spirit of God Like a Fire is Burning." Slides depicting the growth of the church throughout the world may be shown during the song. Slides may begin with Nauvoo era, continue through pioneer trek, temples in various parts of the world, photos of your own ward missionaries, ending with slide depicting Christ.)

(THE END)

Suggested slides to be used for narration:
1. Artists rendition of Mayan empire, or actual photos of glyphs depicting a great mass of people with great cities.
2. Artist rendition or glyphs of Mayan wars.
3. Pictures of ruins in South and Central America.
4. Paintings of 15th century Europe.
5. Picture of a globe or the sea.
6. Painting of Columbus.
7. Picture of Pilgrims landing.
8. Pictures of Indian slaves or colonial Indian wars.
9. Bible or Old and New Testaments
10. Joseph Smith in the Grove
11. Book of Mormon, Pearl of Great Price, Doctrine and Covenants.
12. Christ

Family Frolics, Relief Society Renditions and Sharing Time Skits -- Resource Manual

THE PUMPKIN CHILD

NARRATOR (male or female)
MOTHER
SHARI
3 GIRLS: LITTLE RED, GOLDILOCKS and 3RD GIRL
MURAD
NANA

About 15 mins. Order #4014

NARRATOR: Once there was a mother who very much wanted a child.
MOTHER: I'd give anything to have a child of my own to love and care for. I wouldn't even care if she looked like a pumpkin.
> *(She exits)*

NARRATOR: The mother's wish was answered. Soon afterward she did have a child -- a beautiful girl that she named Shari. But the mother's wish went even further, for after a few days, her beautiful daughter suddenly looked like a pumpkin.
> *(The MOTHER enters and sees the pumpkin in the crib instead of SHARI. She is distressed)*

MOTHER: Oh, my a...a...
> *(she cries)*

What has happened to you? How can I ...?
(MUSIC STARTS)
I must love you no matter what you look like for you are mine.
> DON'T FRET, LITTLE ONE.
> SLEEP TIGHT LITTLE ONE.
> FOR THERE'S A STAR INSIDE YOU,
> THAT SHINES SO BRIGHT TO GUIDE YOU.
> AND THAT IS WHERE YOU'LL FIND
> THE LOVE FOR OTHERS THAT WILL FIND
> IT'S WAY BACK TO YOU -- TO YOU.

> *(MUSIC continues as underscore. During the following MOTHER cares for and then kisses SHARI and sends her off to play.)*

NARRATOR: Over the years the pumpkin child grew and grew. When the child was fifteen, Mother decided to send her off to school with the other girls. As Shari went out into the street, all the neighbors laughed at her from inside their houses.
> *(Laughter from backstage)*

The pumpkin child cried and cried and went back into her house.

MOTHER: Shari, stop crying now and listen. Don't you let other people get you down Now go to school and learn -- reading, writing and 'rithmetic and I'll teach you to knit and cook. Now get along and have fun!

> *(Shari bops on down to the schoolyard. There are three girls walking, laughing and gossiping. At first they ignore Shari.)*

GIRLS: *(Ad lib gossip)*
LITTLE RED: What a terrible color -- orange!
3RD GIRL: Why don't you go back to the pumpkin patch where you belong!

> *(The GIRLS laugh at her and SHARI goes off to a corner by herself. There is a grapevine, and she sticks her arm out of the pumpkin to get a grape. As she does this, MURAD, a Prince, comes up from behind a wall and watches her.)*

MURAD: *(To audience)* Who is this creature? Why her hand and arm are human! I must find out who she is!

> *(SHARI puts her arm out again to get another grape. He grabs her hand to talk with her and she screams, takes her arm back and hurries away.)*

Wait! I only wanted to talk with you! Please -- come back!

> *(He looks in his hand and finds her ring)*

Her ring! I'll go and find the hand that fits this ring and then I will marry her!

(MUSIC IN)

> I'LL GIVE MY LOVE A RING WHEN I FIND HER.
> I'LL GIVE MY LOVE A RING TO REMIND HER --
> THAT I LOVE HER HOW SHE IS
> AND WHO SHE IS
> AND WHAT SHE IS!
> THAT I'M NOT A SIMPLE STRANGER
> OUT TO CHANGE OR REARRANGE HER.
> THAT WHATEVER SHE DOES I'LL BE BEHIND HER
> BUT FIRST I'VE GOT TO FIND HER.

NARRATOR: That was Murad. He is the rich merchant's son. He really fell for Shari, don't you think so? Well, he ran home to his house searching for his servant, Nana.

MURAD: *(Rushing in)* Nana! Nana!
NANA: Yes, yes, Murad. What is it? What's wrong?
MURAD: *(Giving NANA the ring)* Here. It is time that I was married. Go to each house in the town and find the girl whose ring finger fits this ring. Then bring her back to the house to be my bride.

> *(They both exit. The three girls come on and start talking excitedly)*

GOLDILOCKS: Oh! Isn't it exciting! I'm sure that the ring will fit my hand and I will marry the handsome Murad!

3RD GIRL: No! You are much too big and ugly. I shall put my hand out and the ring will slide daintily onto my finger.
LITTLE RED: No, No, No! I will marry Murad!
(They start fighting and squabbling as NANA enters with the ring)
NANA: Girls...girls..GIRLS!
(They stop fighting and look at NANA)
Now that's no way for ladies to act! I've been asked by his lordship Murad, to find the owner of this ring. I've searched every other house in town and I haven't found her. Do you know who the owner is?
GOLDILOCKS: Of course, I am the owner!
LITTLE RED: Me! The ring belongs to me!
3RD GIRL: Let me try it on. I'm sure it's mine!
NANA: Girls! GIRLS! Now, just be quiet and you can all try it on.
(NANA tries it on GOLDILOCKS first and it won't go on no matter how hard she pushes against her pudgy fingers. Then the 3RD GIRL tries it on and her finger is so skinny that it slips right off. And the ring won't fit LITTLE RED either.)
NANA: Isn't there anyone else who should try on the ring? Can you think of anyone I've missed? Anyone?
GOLDILOCKS: If you want a good laugh...
3RD GIRL: And if you're really desperate...
LITTLE RED: You can try the pumpkin in that little house just out of town.
GOLDILOCKS: But I doubt that she'll have a finger to fit the ring!
(All three girls laugh. NANA goes to the little house. MOTHER answers door)
NANA: Is there a young girl living in this house?
MOTHER: I hope you won't be like all the others and laugh at me. But, when I was younger I wished so hard for a little girl of my own that I was sent a pumpkin instead.
NANA: Let me see the pumpkin.
(SHARI enters)
MOTHER: What do you want with my pumpkin child?
NANA: My master, Murad, the merchant's son, has sent me to find a wife for him. He wishes to marry the girl, rich or poor, whose ring finger fits this ring.
(A delicate hand pops out of the pumpkin. They try the ring on and it fits perfectly)
NANA: Come my child, you are the one.
(They leave)
NARRATOR: All the town laughed because the richest and most handsome young man in the whole town was going to marry a fat orange pumpkin. But marry her he did. After the wedding, Murad took his little pumpkin to a

house far away on a hill where he could care for her and never allow others to laugh at her again.

MURAD: *(kisses the pumpkin)* Good night, my sweet, little pumpkin.
> *(As they sleep the pumpkin shell splits open and SHARI emerges and kisses MURAD gently. He wakes.)*

Who are you?
> *(SHARI points to the pumpkin)*

Shari? Shari! What happened? How did you get out?

SHARI: You released me. If you had not loved me when I was a pumpkin, I would not be free of my shell now.
> YOUR LOVE IS THE THING
> THAT RELEASED ME
> AND I STAND HERE FRIGHTENED AND SHY!
> YOUR LOVE AND MY RING,
> THEY RELEASED ME.
> AND NOW I AM WONDERING WHY
> A THING SO SIMPLE HAS SUCH POWER?
> NOW, I BELIEVE IN THE POWER OF LOVE!
>
> *(They embrace)*

NARRATOR: And so Murad and his beautiful pumpkin wife, Shari, lived happily for many, many years. They kept the pumpkin shell in a corner of their house to remind them of the days when Murad had loved his wife even though everyone else had laughed at her and them. The most interesting thing about life must be that each of us needs to feel wanted just for who we are. Not for what we can do or how we look. You, your parents, even the person sitting next to you wants to feel wanted!
> *(Cast enters stage to sing)*

ALL:
> NOW WE UNDERSTAND WHY
> A THING SO SIMPLE HAS SUCH POWER!
> LOVE IS WHAT WE ARE MADE OF.
> THE FRACTION OF A TINT OR A CHADE OF
> THE COLORS OF THE EARTH ARE ARRAYED WITH LOVE!

(THE END)

SOCKY AT THE DENTIST

1 Sock Puppet with eyes
1 Toothy Puppet with eyes

SOCKY: Oh, hi. Are you all waiting here for the Dentist? Hey, take it from me, just get out of here quick before he sees you! I just came in with a little toothache -- hardly anything at all -- and he yanked out all my teeth! Every single one -- see?
TOOTHY: Hi, Shrimp. How do you like my beautiful teeth?
SOCKY: You'll be talking out the other side of your face after you go in there.
TOOTHY: Oh! I just came out!
  (He chomps his new teeth and starts away)
SOCKY: Hey, come back here! Those are my teeth! Give them back right now!
  (TOOTHY dissappears)
Yeah, and I bet you get your hair from a barber! How am I supposed to scare anyone without any teeth? You see, underneath this mild-mannered exterior, I'm a wild beast! I'm as ferocious as a Bulldog! I'm as terrible as a fire-breathing dragon! Auuuggghhh! Do I see singed eyebrows? Oh, but nobody will believe I'm dangerous when I don't have any teeth! I can't very well mouth people to death! I know! I'll become a great sword fighter. That way I can keep my mouth shut! But I'd probably swallow the sword, and then wouldn't I look funny? Maybe I can be a ventriloquist. If I talk out of the side of my mouth I'll be able to fool them all. Oh, but what I really want to be is a famous opera star!
  (He takes a deep breath, during which a fly buzzes past, circles his head, then flies into his mouth. He snaps his mouth shut, there is a brief internal battle, then he swallows, groans in distaste, and disappears.)
  THE END

FAMILY COUNCIL IN HEAVEN

HEAVENLY FATHER
HEAVENLY MOTHER
JESUS
LUCIFER
 FIVE CHILDREN (or more, if desired)
(Can be done with puppets or with persons)

SCENE ONE: *Heavenly Mother is on stage wearing an apron and standing over a big pot of stew. Heavenly Father enters and begins talking to her.*

HEAVENLY FATHER: *(Clearing throat says)* Well, well. Its time to call the children.
HEAVENLY MOTHER: But I haven't gotten dinner ready yet.
HEAVENLY FATHER: Oh, I'm sorry dear, I didn't mean right now. I meant after dinner; It's time for family council.
HEAVENLY MOTHER: *(leaning out towards the audience as if thinking, to herself)* What's it about in tonight?.
HEAVENLY FATHER: I thought we would talk to our children about school.
HEAVENLY MOTHER: School?
HEAVENLY FATHER: Yes. The earth school that soon will be finished.
HEAVENLY MOTHER: *(with a sigh)* I guess they are getting old enough to go away to school.
HEAVENLY FATHER: They are quite grown up now.
HEAVENLY MOTHER: I just wish they wouldn't grow so fast.
HEAVENLY FATHER: I know it will not be easy for you to have the children leave home and go away to the earth.
HEAVENLY MOTHER: It certainly won't be easy to send them so far away from their heavenly home.
HEAVENLY FATHER: But they will be happy on earth. They will be happy studying and learning new things.
HEAVENLY MOTHER: Yes it will be good to see them learn. I will miss them. But they must have the chance to learn.
HEAVENLY FATHER: I too, will miss them. But they will be able to call us when they pray.
HEAVENLY MOTHER: I certainly hope they call us every night before they go to bed.
HEAVENLY FATHER: They are very good children. They will remember to say their prayers.

HEAVENLY MOTHER: Well, I'd best finish dinner on so that we can have the Family Council.

SCENE TWO: Heavenly Father and Heavenly Mother are to the right of the stage and the rest of the children are to the center and left of stage.

HEAVENLY FATHER: Is everyone here?
HEAVENLY MOTHER: I think all the children are here.
HEAVENLY FATHER: Well, I'm glad everyone is here. I have some important plans to tell you about.
1st CHILD: What kind of plans?
2nd CHILD: *(politely)* Sh... and you'll find out.
LUCIFER: Yeah, be quiet so we can find out about the plans.
HEAVENLY MOTHER: Now children, listen so your Father can tell you all His plans.
HEAVENLY FATHER: Since all of you have grown up I would like to give you the chance of going away to school.
1st CHILD: What School?
2nd CHILD: *(politely)* Sh... and you'll find out.
LUCIFER: Yeah, be quiet so we can find out!
HEAVENLY FATHER: The school is the earth school, that soon will be built.
3rd CHILD: Where will that be?
HEAVENLY FATHER: The earth school will be a long way away. But it is a place where you can learn many new things, have new experiences.
4th CHILD: I like to learn'
3rd CHILD: So do I.
1st CHILD: Who will teach us?
2nd CHILD: *(politely)* Sh... and you'll find out.
LUCIFER: Yeah, be quiet so we can find out.
HEAVENLY FATHER: A leader will be chosen and he will send teacher's to teach you.
LUCIFER: A Leader?
HEAVENLY FATHER: Yes, a leader. Someone that will teach you the right things to do. The things that will lead you back to your heavenly home.
1st CHILD: What will happen to those who don't follow the leader?
2nd CHILD: *(politely)* Sh....You ask too many questions.
LUCIFER: Yeah, why don't you be quiet!
HEAVENLY FATHER: She asked a very good question. Those who don't follow the leader may get lost and won't know how to find their way home.
3rd CHILD: That would be terrible!
HEAVENLY FATHER: Yes, it would be terrible. But the leader would choose teachers that will help each child find the right way.
LUCIFER: Who is going to be the leader?

HEAVENLY FATHER: It will have to be someone who can teach, guide and lead.
LUCIFER: You mean someone that has a big stick and can make everyone do what is right?!
HEAVENLY FATHER: No, Lucifer, it must be someone that will let them choose for themselves which way they want to go.
LUCIFER: Well, I think the leader should have a big stick.
HEAVENLY FATHER: The leader must also be willing to suffer and die for the mistakes of others.
LUCIFER: Well that's silly. If you use a big stick nobody is going to make any foolish mistakes.
HEAVENLY FATHER: But if you use a big stick, nobody will know how good it feels to choose the right.
JESUS: Father is right. If we are made to do everything we won't learn how to choose the good things.
HEAVENLY FATHER: That's correct. You must have your freedom to do those things that make you happy or sad.
LUCIFER: I still say the leader needs a big stick.
HEAVENLY FATHER: Why? Lucifer?
LUCIFER: So the leader can make everyone follow him.
HEAVENLY FATHER: If you force people to do the right thing there are many who would not learn. We learn best by correcting our own mistakes.
4th CHILD: Father is right.
3rd CHILD: Yes, He is.
JESUS: Father's plan is best. We must have a leader who will show us the right way, but let us choose.
HEAVENLY FATHER: Well, Whom shall I send to be the Leader?
JESUS: Here am I, send me.
LUCIFER: Don't send him, send me!
HEAVENLY FATHER: I shall send Jesus, my first born.
LUCIFER: Well, I'm going to find a big stick and knock some sense into someone!
HEAVENLY FATHER: Lucifer, I think you should go to your room until you change your behavior.
LUCIFER: Ah...bu...bu...
4th CHILD: Now, how many of you want Jesus to be our leader?
All the **CHILDREN:** We all do.
HEAVENLY FATHER: (*nodding and smiling*) Family Council is over with until tomorrow night.
CHILDREN: Yeah! Jesus is our leader!

SCENE THREE: *The children and Jesus are all gathered and waiting.*

3rd CHILD: Are we going to have family council tonight?
JESUS: Yes, Father said we were.
4th CHILD: I'm sure happy we picked you to be the leader.
JESUS: I hope I can be a good leader.
5th CHILD: You will. I know you will.
2nd CHILD: Sh...here they come now.
HEAVENLY FATHER: Good, you are here.
1st CHILD: Are we going to have family council tonight, Father?
2nd CHILD: Sh...
HEAVENLY FATHER: Yes... I... dear, we are.
ALL CHILDREN: Good! Hurray! I'm excited.
HEAVENLY FATHER: Well now, lets begin.
5th CHILD: Can we begin by singing our favorite song?
HEAVENLY FATHER: Yes, that would be nice. Jesus, would you lead us?
JESUS: Ready, begin.
CHILDREN: I AM A CHILD OF GOD AND HE HAS CALLED ME HERE.
HAS GIVEN ME A HEAVENLY HOME
WITH PARENTS KIND AND DEAR.
LEAD ME, GUIDE ME WALK BESIDE ME,
HELP ME FIND THE WAY.
TEACH ME ALL THAT I MUST KNOW
TO BE LIKE HIM SOMEDAY.
HEAVENLY FATHER: Thank you children, that was special.
HEAVENLY MOTHER: Yes, it always means a lot to your Father and I when you sing that song.
HEAVENLY FATHER: Now children, last night, Jesus was chosen to be your leader. How do you feel about that?
ALL CHILDREN: We want Jesus to be our leader.
HEAVENLY FATHER: That's,very good! Jesus how do you feel about that?
JESUS: I will be happy to teach them and show them the way back home.
HEAVENLY FATHER: You understand that you will be asked to suffer and die for the mistakes of others?
JESUS: Yes, Father, I understand.
HEAVENLY FATHER: I know you will do a good job.
JESUS: I know I must not fail. I must be a good leader to help my brothers and sisters find the way home.
HEAVENLY FATHER: You will have teachers to help you.
JESUS: Yes, and they must be the best teachers I can find.
HEAVENLY FATHER: Now, Jesus, you will need the Priesthood power. So that you can build the earth school and be the leader.
JESUS: Yes, Father, I will need the priesthood power.

HEAVENLY FATHER: Well, come with me so that I may give you the priesthood power.
>*(Heavenly Father and Jesus leave main stage. They go behind the scrim curtain and reappear on the top of the puppet stage.)*

HEAVENLY FATHER: Now that you have the priesthood power I must send you out there to find the materials to build the earth school.

JESUS: I shall find the materials and build the earth school.

HEAVENLY FATHER: Come back as soon as you have finished.

JESUS: I shall be back.
>*(Music crescendos and stage curtains remain closed for 1 minute. Jesus reappears at the top of the puppet stage.)*

JESUS: I'm back!
>*(Heavenly Father appears)*

I finished the earth school.

HEAVENLY FATHER: Yes. I was watching. You have done a good job. Come, lets call the children together and we shall show them what you have done. Blow the bugle!
>*(Horn is sounded. Curtain reopens and Heavenly Father and Jesus reenter on the main stage. All the children are there except for a couple.)*

5th CHILD: I'm coming I'm coming;

HEAVENLY MOTHER: The children arc all here.

HEAVENLY FATHER: Come children and see the earth school that Jesus has made for you.
>*(The bugle is sounded behind the audience by an angel in white. The audience turns to see an angel an a screen used for showing slides.)*

HEAVENLY FATHER: There's the earth. There's the Sun, moon and stars.

CHILDREN: (variously) There's the land and water.
There's the mountains.
There's the ocean.
There's the trees and plants.
There's the flowers.
There's the birds.
There's the fishes.
There's the animals.
and there's the earth school.

ALL CHILDREN: Yeah for Jesus our leader.
Yeah for the earth school.
Now we can learn.
Hooray for Jesus our leader.

(THE END)

ORDER FORM

Your Ward or Stake: _____

Your Name: _____

Your Address: _____

Your City, State Zip: _____

Your E-mail Address: _____

Your Phone Number: _____

(Place a check mark in the blank of the title(s) desired.)

- _____ **AND THAT'S THE WAY IT WAS** -- Order # 4001 $7.50
- _____ **THE EXAMPLE** -- Order # 4002. $5.00
- _____ **FUNSMOKE** -- Order # 4003. $7.50
- _____ **THE IGI CAPER** -- Order # 4004. $7.50
- _____ **JONAH AND THE BIG FISH** -- Order # 4005. $5.00
- _____ **LET FREEDOM RING** -- Order # 4006. $10.00
- _____ **MALADIES PECULIAR TO THE MORMON FAITH** -- Order # 4007. $5.00
- _____ **NEPHI AND LABAN** -- Order # 4008. $7.50
- _____ **THE NO TALENT** -- Order # 4009. $5.00
- _____ **PIONEER CHILDREN** -- Order # 4010. $10.00
- _____ **THE RELUCTANT SHEPHERD** -- Order # 4011. $10.00
- _____ **VISITING TEACHING LEADER** -- Order # 4012. $5.00
- _____ **A VOICE FROM THE DUST** -- Order # 4013. $10.00
- _____ **THE PUMPKIN CHILD** -- Order # 4014. $10.00
- _____ **SOCKY AT THE DENTIST** -- Order # 4015. $3.00
- _____ **FAMILY COUNCIL IN HEAVEN** -- Order # 4016. $7.50

The PayPal Shopping Cart will add Utah Sales Tax to every order. Do NOT enter your zipcode or you will be charged for shipping; and there is nothing to ship.

Send a check to:
Zion Theatricals
3877 W. Leicester Bay
South Jordan, UT 84095
(We will wait until the check clears your bank before sending the PDF file)
OR call:
801-550-7741
801-282-8159
OR send a PayPal payment to our email address for the total amount due:
cmichaeperry53@gmail.com

www.ingramcontent.com/pod-product-compliance
Lightning Source LLC
Chambersburg PA
CBHW071322040426
42444CB00009B/2065